THE CRAFTS OF MALAYSIA

FRONT AND BACK COVER:
OGIVAL GOLD BELT
BUCKLE, SEE PAGE 196–99
(TARA SOSROWARDOYO/
MUZIUM NEGARA
COLLECTION).
FRONT COVER INSETS:
DETAIL OF *SUNGKIT*
BADGE, SEE PAGE 153
(LAWRENCE LIM/KEDIT
HEIRLOOM COLLECTION);
WOODEN-HILTED KRIS
AND SHEATH CARVED BY
NORHAIZAH NORDIN,
KG. RAJA BESUT,
TERENGGANU
(HALIM STUDIO).
BACK COVER: KITE FROM
KELANTAN, SEE PAGE 223
(KRAFTANGAN).

ENDPAPERS: RICHLY
WOVEN SONGKET CLOTH
FROM THE ATELIER OF
YM TENGKU ISMAIL BIN
TENGKU SU,
TERENGGANU.

FRONTISPIECE: A ROYAL
FIVE-LAYERED
CEREMONIAL MAT OF
WOVEN PANDANUS
LEAVES COVERED WITH
EMBROIDERY, WITH
PERIMETER OF EACH
LAYER DECORATED WITH
FINELY WOVEN SONGKET.

5: CLOSE-UP OF FOUR
BEAUTIFUL MODERN
FINGER RINGS WITH
DIFFERENT PRECIOUS AND
SEMI-PRECIOUS STONE
SETTINGS.

6-7: SARAWAK CRAFTS, IN
AN ILLUSTRATION FROM
F. RATZEL, *THE HISTORY
OF MANKIND*, VOL. 1,
LONDON, 1898.

10-11: A SELECTION
OF OLD AND
CONTEMPORARY MALAY
AND PERANAKAN
SILVERWARE EMBELLISHED
WITH EXQUISITE
DESIGNS, CIRCA 1800 TO
THE PRESENT TIME.

Editorial Advisory Board

Dato' Haji Sulaiman Othman
Director-General
Malaysian Handicraft Development Corporation

Tuan Haji Mohd Zulkifli bin Haji Abdul Aziz
Director-General, Muzium Negara, Malaysia

Puan Azah Aziz, well-known writer and
expert on costumes and textiles

Puan Marina Mahathir
Mosaique Communications Sdn Bhd

Peter Schoppert, Editions Didier Millet

Authors

Dato' Haji Sulaiman Othman
Haji Rudin Salinger
Khoo Joo Ee
Mohd Kassim Haji Ali
Patricia Regis
Yeoh Jin Leng

with supplementary texts by
Dr Siti Zainon Ismail and Vernon Art Kedit

Introduction and text on tekat embroidery
translated from Malay by Razif Bahari

Photographers

Abdul Halim Mohd Noor
Tommy Chang
Dennis Lau
Tara Sosrowardoyo

with additional photography by
Ibrahim Ahmad and Lawrence Lim

Commissioning Editor
Peter Schoppert

Editor
Shamira Bhanu

Design Concept
Ko Hui Huy of Duet Design Pte Ltd

Designer
Tan Tat Ghee, EDM

The Crafts of Malaysia
© Editions Didier Millet 1994
593 Havelock Road, #02-01/02 Isetan Office
Building, Singapore 169641

First published 1994
Reprinted with corrections 1997

Colour separation by Colourscan, Singapore
Printed in Singapore by Tien Wah Press

ISBN 981-3018-07-0

THE CRAFTS
OF MALAYSIA

THIS BOOK HAS BEEN MADE POSSIBLE
THANKS TO THE ACTIVE SUPPORT OF
OUR SPONSORS.

 -Marconi

TEXTILES 108

Khoo Joo Ee
with essay on embroidery by Siti Zainon Ismail
and essay on Iban textiles by Vernon Art Kedit

METALS 162

Mohd Kassim Haji Ali

OTHER 216
CRAFTS

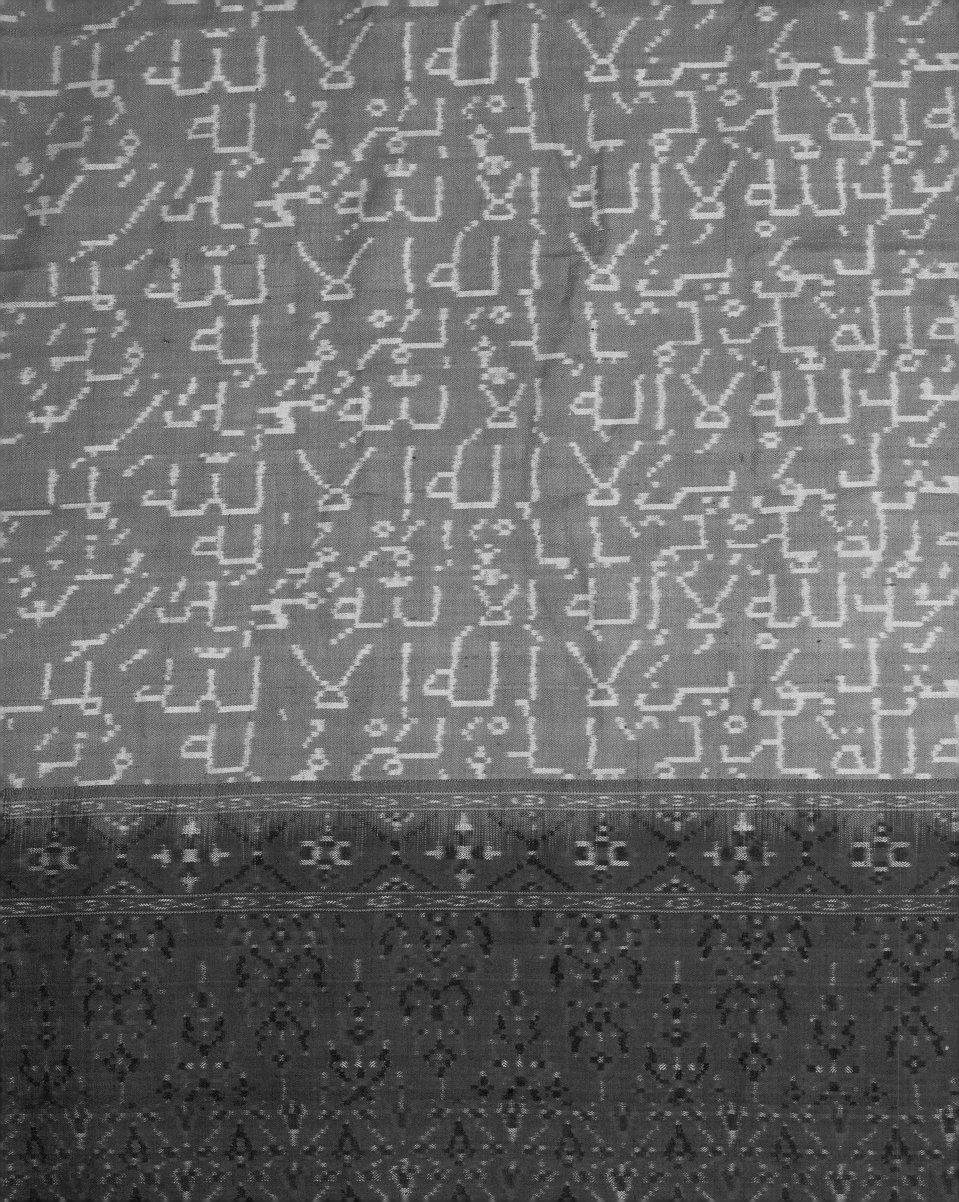

INTRODUCTION

I t's not the garb of today's kings
but those bygones of yesteryears
hang it to dry and it will retain
its lustre
soak it and it will remain preserved
a little tear only adds to its character
that will not diminish but enhance
this treasure
one hundred rial in thread it costs —
speckled with a dewdrop
its cubit-long thread in a whorl
till the south wind comes to blow it
unwound!

Even in translation, the above extract from a *gurindam* (verse) by a *penglipur lara* (a soother of sorrows or story teller) in the *Seri Rama Melayu* from Perak eloquently expresses a cultural, aesthetic and intellectual sensibility that is powerfully cadenced, subtly nuanced and unmistakably Malaysian.

This *gurindam*, with its elegance of form, allusiveness and richness of phrase, has a resonance which reflects the depth of a people's psyche — their refined sensibilities, gentility, fortitude, dignity, proud politeness, keen observation, deep-delving spirituality and tenacity of conviction.

Malaysian arts and crafts, even as a common reference point and source of unity, cannot presume the erasure of internal differences and particularities. Malaysia's cultural fabric today is derived from a welter of vast cultural hinterlands, particularly from the many tribes and societies of the Malay Archipelago, each widely divergent in its social, political, economic, spiritual and aesthetic way of life. Such diversity adds to the repertoire of modes of cultural expressions that can be included under the rubric of "Malaysianness". It is precisely this complexity and flexibility which makes up the vitality of Malaysia's cultures.

This creative tension and sensibility are derived in part from the cultures of the *kaum asli* or indigenous tribes. The *kaum asli* are known for their sense of aesthetic beauty and their real and/or symbolic ties to nature. Their intimate affinity with their natural milieu, together with their animistic beliefs and their proclivity for the supernatural, have inspired many traditional artefacts found in this country.

FACING PAGE:
MALAYSIA'S CRAFT
TRADITION IS STRONGLY
ALLIED TO A SOUND
RELIGIOUS FRAMEWORK
INFLUENCED BY ISLAM,
AS CAN BE SEEN IN THIS
TEXTILE, WHICH IS
PATTERNED IN JAWI
CALLIGRAPHY.
THIS PAGE:
AN OCTAGONAL
GOLD COIN ISSUED BY
SULTAN ABDUL JALIL
SHAH III (1623-1677) OF
JOHOR. THE DENOMINA-
TION OF THIS COIN IS
KNOWN AS "MAS"
AND IT WEIGHS ABOUT
2.45 GRAMS OF
PURE GOLD.

A SPIRIT FIGURE SUCH
AS THIS IS A CARVING
OF THE BIDAYUH. IT
COULD BE EITHER MALE
OR FEMALE AND WAS
PLACED AT THE
ENTRANCE OF A VILLAGE
TO WARD OFF EVIL
SPIRITS. IT WAS USED
DURING THE SPIRIT
FESTIVAL, HELD FOR
ALL THOSE WHO HAVE
DIED SINCE THE
PREVIOUS FESTIVAL.

The Malays, on their part, have provided a collective sense of aesthetic beauty based on the belief that beauty itself is related to divine power and God's infinite riches; a sense that is constant in most of their works, one allied to a strong religious framework influenced by Islam and the teachings of the Holy Quran.

The cultures of the Chinese and the Indians as well as other migrant races like the Portuguese have proved attractive sources of nourishment. The various tribes in Sabah and Sarawak are other constituents that add yet more colours to the vivid compendium that is Malaysian arts and crafts. It is this access to worlds so richly varied and so polymorphous, as well as the stimulation of a multiracial milieu, freedom of thought, religious choice, belief, and the latitude given to creative expressions, which explains the matrix of diversity, modes of thinking, choice of forms and various creative inspirations that make up Malaysian handicraft works.

The *gurindam* of the *penglipur lara* above extols, without self-praise, the works of Malaysia's craftspeople as an achievement of a high order. Almost without exception, local craftworks not only reflect fine craftsmanship but the success of their creators in capturing the subtle nuances of local aesthetics.

"Hang it to dry and it will retain its lustre/ soak it and it will remain preserved". The beauty of the Malay silk weave, so delicately embroidered and finely stitched as to look lustrous and resplendent, wet or dry, is one of the unique aspects of Malaysian handicrafts which the *penglipur lara* captures succinctly in his *gurindam*.

The power of the language reflects the profound and refined sensibility with which craftsmen and women embrace their crafts. It reflects their devotion to quality, one exercised with an awareness of the aesthetic imperatives of their own creative medium.

It will be patent to the reader of this *gurindam*, and the reality it evokes, that the craftwork of weaving being described here and the philosophy of its practitioners provide a helpful entry into the heart of the culture's sensibility.

Craft as a totemic symbol of a culture's presiding spirit and sensibility embodies not only that people's way of life, ideolect and *weltanschauung*, but the inner sanctum of their psyche and the bedrock of their enduring values.

History has proven a crucial fructifying force in the development of these crafts. The Malay Peninsula, which in the 1960's became part of the political entity we now know as Malaysia, lies in a strategic geographical position served by the Straits of Melaka, a sea passage of paramount importance for maritime trade. Trade and prosperity heralded a concomitant cultural unfolding and ferment which first gave rise to ancient kingdoms such as Langkasuka and Kataha and later the Melaka Sultanate. As one of the earliest nation states in the Malay Archipelago, Melaka became a meeting place for traders from the Indian subcontinent, West Asia and China as early as the 13th century.

The burgeoning traffic of trade brought with it edifying cultural influences which were assimilated and accepted by the local people. These cultural inheritances, however diverse, became harmonised to form a common heritage which ensured a historical and cultural continuity. The advent of Islam not only sustained these varying influences, but enriched and expanded their scope. Islamic values, which are the organising principles that bind the country together even today, helped preserve the cultural heritages which the presence of migrant communities served to foster rather than dilute.

More than just cultural artefacts, craftworks became precious commodities which commanded high value as goods for trade. Not surprisingly, local handicraft works received royal patronage from the Malay kings, flourishing particularly in Kelantan, Terengganu, Kedah and Perak. Skilled craftsmen like goldsmiths, silversmiths and wood carvers were as much a part of ancient court culture as the *kris*, betrothal cups, betel nut bowls, wooden decorative wall panels and other ornate palace regalia which they produced.

Today's new *zeitgeist* has brought radical change. Amidst the dialectics of social and political change that a young nation like Malaysia has undergone, the primary creative impulses of local craftsmen have shifted somewhat. This is evident if we look at the craftworks currently available in the open market today. Craftworks in contemporary settings have to cater to a clientèle whose tastes are fashioned by years of exposure to foreign imports, high-quality novelty items and new materials. Craftsmen are well aware that, despite its excellence and unique styles, the local handicraft enterprise would be difficult to keep alive unless they updated and enhanced their techniques and skills.

Towards the first half of the 20th century, the growth of local handicraft works was seriously retarded in the face of stiff competition from these foreign imports. Domestic demand for local textiles plummeted

as a result of a deluge of imported fabrics flooding the local market, stirring great uncertainties for a time amongst local silk weavers and embroiderers alike, giving cause for concern about their future. Similar challenges were to face silver- and coppersmiths as well.

The fifties, however, saw a resurgence in the development of handicrafts commensurate with the ensuing socio-economic developments that took place in the country during this period.

This progress gave a new direction to the course of crafts in Malaysia. As mentioned earlier, multifarious richness and refined sensibility are among the outstanding hallmarks of Malaysian crafts. One of the most interesting strands of this colourful tapestry is perhaps the aesthetic values and sensibilities exhibited by the orang asli, the indigenous people of Malaysia. If one studies the handicrafts of the Mah Meri society inhabiting the coastal areas of Selangor and the Jah Hut society in the mountainous region of Jerantut, Pahang, one would find two different expressions of aesthetic sensibility —both equally unique yet similar in their deep-rootedness in traditional culture, religious beliefs and their concomitants. Their wood carvings, for example, clearly reflect the powerful influence their natural surroundings exert on their craft's creation and conception.

We discern in the Mah Meri's and Jah Hut's conception of their crafts a sensibility linked to the natural landscape, the flora and the fauna which inform and infuse nearly all their works. Sea, sky, river, the climate, the nature of the soil, the physiognomy of plants and animals and the view of beautiful nature are all harmoniously absorbed and made part of their creative thoughts and feelings.

The harmony results, in this case, from attuning culture to nature in a way that elicits an awareness and respect for ecological forces. We are struck by the orang asli's feeling of oneness with creation and his sense of the beauty of nature, celebrated in the very act of recognising his fragile existence in relation to nature's indomitable and omnipotent power.

In their origin and the way they are formed, both the art and sensibility of the orang asli derive from a powerful sense of a belief which sanctifies nature. Many of the themes, motifs, images and forms used in their handicrafts are modelled after the bounty of nature around them. For instance, images of sea-dwelling creatures and animals that can be found in river mouths are prevalent in wood carvings produced by the Mah Meri, while the carvings, sculptures, statues and figurines made by the Jah Hut are mostly representations of animals like monkeys, tigers and elephants. These patterns of recurring images and motifs are used with special potency by the Jah Huts and Mah Meris, and are intrinsic to their way of seeing and ordering their world view.

Nature and the environment have become a presiding muse and inspiration, a crucible from which craftworks assume their shape, form and style. In short, it is generally true to say that Malaysian crafts take their special form and content in dialectical synthesis with the diverse local conditions in which the various communities find themselves situated. For the Mah Meri and Jah Hut tribes, renowned for their dextrous skills and fine craftsmanship, these forms and motifs have become a distinctive trait of their crafts since time immemorial.

The propensity to produce works of fine quality and workmanship with the most basic and simple of tools is also another point worth noting. Some of the crafts featured in this book are produced by using common basic implements like the knife, for example, or through relatively simple processes like weaving or tying. The resulting objects, intended for everyday use, are basic in their functions but meticulously and beautifully constructed.

That such crude and rudimentary creative media could be used to accomplish such sophisticated and refined handicrafts is demonstrated also in works by other tribes of orang asli, like the Senoi, Sakai and Jakun.

These tribes' rich traditions and sensibilities have been known to distil craftworks of inordinate beauty. A variety of ethnic handicrafts, such as carved dagger hilts, blowpipes, woven tribal baskets and rattan or bamboo bags are not only produced as cultural items but, more importantly, as objects for daily use.

Among other creative works produced by the orang asli, their cave drawings and etchings stand significantly as testimony to their artistic consciousness and sensibility of their fertile natural surroundings. These works, though primitive in nature but no less captivating for being so, bear important historical and anthropological significance. It is important to bear in mind that the forms of tribal crafts have a close nexus with the tribe's socio-ecological environment and their means of livelihood. Sources of livelihood differ: some people practise food gathering and hunting while others agricultural farming and fishing, or a mixture of any of these combinations.

Tribal crafts in this respect are produced to complement such activities. For example, contraptions such as bamboo fish traps and snares for capturing animals are created primarily for a practical purpose: to facilitate the hunter's search for food.

The same can be said of handicrafts produced by the many hundreds of tribal people living in Sabah and Sarawak, who can be divided into two broad categories based on their natural environment and their livelihood practices.

For those living near rivers, deltas, river mouths and lakes, or by the coastal areas, water is both a creative and physical lifeline. Sea, rain, flood plains, silt, swamp and the innumerable life forms they support provide a cosmic backdrop against which destiny is unfolded. In content, style and form, the crafts of these coastal peoples remain noticeably influenced by their geography and landscape.

Fables of identity and systems of mythology, and their manifestation in idols, emblems and totems, arose out of the land that nourishes its inhabitants. The ebb and flow of the river and the sea, and the contours of rocks and crevices, become part of the totality of the tribal peoples' aesthetic consciousness, a correlative of their creative sensibility.

If one observes their craftwork, one notices it takes the form of basic but essential tools of survival which the tribal people use to eke out a living and to trap food for daily sustenance. Such objects include fish traps, and cane or bamboo baskets for catching mussels, crabs and prawns.

These contraptions are made with such fastidious craftsmanship and exceptional quality as to be examplars of refined tribal handwork. In these works, function and creative form are intimately intertwined with each other, with nature as the determinant — the point of departure and the point of return.

It is not surprising, therefore, that motifs of aquatic life forms such as prawns, fish, crabs and crocodiles prevail in the crafts of coastal dwellers, especially among the Orang Laut in Sabah. These dominant images and motifs are the result of their creators' acute sensibility and reconciliation to nature and are held in an equation that develops a certain existential acknowledgment — almost reverence — of the fauna and flora which make up an integral part of their lives.

The same can be said of tribes living in other geographical terrains, like hilly, mountainous or forested areas. Here, again, we need to recognise the different influences exerted by the natural environment and livelihood practices on the formation of identity in the handicrafts of ethnic people. Hill, mountain and forest tribes, for example, utilise different materials and tools, motifs and images for their crafts from those used by their coastal and river brethren.

What we have been dwelling on so far are the domestic factors which have shaped the particular wefts and warps of ethnic Malaysian crafts. When we shift our attention to the present age, however, it becomes salutary to mention the potent forces of external influence on the development of crafts in Malaysia.

If one were to glance at the range of handicrafts made by local craftsmen today, what seems striking is the rapidity with which indigenous forms and styles have yielded to various transformations effected by influences like commercial viability and the demands and specifications of market forces. Trade, commerce and mercantilism have irrevocably left their impact on the local craft scene, ushering in change in terms of the appearance and form of crafts produced.

Like any other great culture, Malaysian cultural sensibility is firmly grounded in tradition, and yet it is able to add to that tradition, to modify and embellish it, in a way that guarantees it vitality and perennial appeal.

A case in point can be seen in the development of the *kain pua* of the Iban of Sarawak. Once a paraphernalia used in religious rituals, redolent with images and motifs depicting the sacred icons and pantheon of local beliefs, the decorations on the *kain pua* have now been somewhat simplified stylistically. And to pander to the taste and demand of today's craft consumers, the material itself is now used to make more temporal things like handbags, jackets and other such items.

In principle, nevertheless, the *kain pua* has kept intact its emblematic high quality and identity. Like in the old days, the fabric is still made by means of the traditional back strap loom and still retains its characteristic mahogany colour, and its vocabulary of images and representations of human, animal and foliage forms.

While the choice of earthy colours, such as mahogany and terracotta, clearly reflects the Iban's affinity and consanguinity with Mother Earth, the fine craftsmanship and meticulous weaving technique manifested in the *kain pua* distinctively puts it on a high pedestal as a craft that all Malaysians can take pride in.

In places where the vegetation is lush and pervaded with the prodigious growth of bamboo, bamboo-based handicrafts have flourished with equal verve. For people living in such areas, bamboo plays a central role in their lives, not only as a primary material for their crafts, but more importantly as a basic resource for everyday use in making tools, common household items and so on. As a society born into this "bamboo culture", Malaysians have produced many unique handicrafts based on bamboo. It could be said that bamboo has profoundly shaped and influenced a wide range of crafts that are found in Malaysia even today.

A nation with a multiracial, multilingual and multicultural mix, Malaysia also boasts craftworks that originate from other rich and more ancient cultures. The Chinese, Indian and other migrant communities are responsible for bringing in these diverse traditions, from which Malaysian crafts have gainfully drawn upon and synthesised, fostering that remarkable creative ferment which inspires many of the works we see today.

Many of the handicrafts created by these migrant communities take the form of objects which are used for rites, rituals and customs associated with their respective religious and communal beliefs.

The earthen wares of the Indian community in Selangor, for example, are produced mostly for use in religious rituals like worships, funerals and religious festivities.

For the Chinese, their most distinctive craft forms are perhaps best represented by the Peranakans, whose lineage in Malaysia dates back more than 600 years. The Peranakan or Straits-born Chinese, whose ancestors came to Melaka to trade silks, precious gems and opium with Arab, Indian and Javanese merchants, have evolved a unique blend of handicrafts which reflect a syncretism of local Malay and Chinese cultures. The munificence of Peranakan arte-facts and the elegant, sometimes ostentatious display of their forms are best seen in their traditional wedding trousseaux. Ornate silver belts, hairpins, beadwork, bracelets, wedding slippers, bed hangings, silver *sireh* boxes and pillow-end plates are part of the grandeur of the *baba* and *nonya* wedding ceremony.

For the Malays, Islam plays an overriding factor in suffusing their sensibility with a deep sense of value for creativity and resourcefulness. The Prophet Muhammad (peace be upon him), in a *hadith* (the Prophet's Traditions) recounted by Imam Ahmad, once said: "The most blessed means to earn thy living is by the work of thine own hands."

Islam extols beauty, which is why in their origin and the way they are formed, the handicrafts produced by the Muslims reflect a religiosity in which beauty is sanctified.

Islam wields a profound influence on the Malaysian ethos and perme-ates every aspect of life in this country. The Muslim community, like all the other art-loving and creative communities in Malaysia, has contributed significantly to the local handicraft scene. The adoption of Islamic values has given their craftwork a powerful presence, a sensitiveness and pathos which — coupled with their fine craftsmanship — gives it its compelling and distinctive character.

Islam, too, has shaped and given colour to the customs and rituals practised and celebrated by the local Malay community. While they embraced the rituals and ceremonies which originated from the parent tradition of the Muslim traders who first brought Islam to this part of the world, they also added to them their own local flavour. A traditional Malay marriage, for example, involves several customary rituals or procedures which must be closely observed.

It starts with the *merisik* (the sending of an envoy or messenger to the prospective bride-to-be's home to enquire whether she is 'available' and interested in marriage), and culmi-nates in the *bersanding* (the ceremony in which both the bride and bride-groom finally get to sit side by side on the bridal dais).

Such elaborate rituals naturally give rise to a set of paraphernalia and ceremonial appurtenances which are used and created according to the dictates of the norms and mores practised. Such artefacts, imbued with Islamic values, form some of the most significant contributions of the Malay/Muslim community to the range of handicrafts in Malaysia.

Many of these artefacts are influ-enced by the many shapes, forms and models offered by nature. For exam-ple, the *labu sayong* (water calabash), an earthernware container decorated with foliage motifs that takes its shape after the gourd or starfruit, is used as a receptacle for keeping water that has been blessed with incanta-tions or as part of the paraphernalia used in rituals performed during a traditional cure.

THIS KENYAH MASK PAINTED IN BLACK, WHITE AND RED WITH SEPARATELY CARVED EARS ATTACHED TO THE FACE WITH ROTAN, IS PRIMARILY USED DURING THE HARVEST FESTIVAL. SOMETIMES SUCH MASKS ARE ALSO USED AS A CEREMONIAL DISGUISE WHEN GREETING UNKNOWN VISITORS TO THE LONGHOUSE.

Embroidery, or *tekatan*, which takes the form of gold thread woven on a base fabric of velvet or brocade, is another local craft which is renowned for its fine craftsmanship. The art of Malay embroidery involves a method of patterning or design characterised by needlework in relief, raised from the surface of velvet and sewn over a filling of *mempulur* (usually made of paper, a type of rattan or pieces of bamboo).

This handicraft, well-known for its magnificent stitchwork, is traditionally associated with, and used for, decorations during wedding ceremonies and other traditional Malay functions. Floor mats, pillowcases, beautifully adorned *tepak sirih* (commodes or chests where betel leaves are kept or displayed) and other traditional items are known to have elaborately embroidered decorations which form part of the pomp and splendour of Malay custom.

The same dazzling skill and resplendent craftwork which have become a hallmark of Malay handicrafts can also be seen in the art of weaving. Exhibiting an intricate but harmonious interlacing of both gold and multicoloured threads in exquisite designs based on plant, fruit, flower and bird motifs, the *kain songket* reveals the Malay community's keen sensibility towards their natural environment.

The *pucuk rebung* (bamboo shoots), *siku keluang* ("flying fox's elbow", so-called because the motifs form acute angles) and *tampok manggis* (mangosteen calyx) motifs are among the myriad of delicate and flowing nature-inspired patterns, designs and motifs used in both the making of *kain songket* as well as batik. An example of this type of handicraft is the fine weavework of Pahang.

Among the activities that are still being practised as part of the repertoire of Malay craftwork heritage is the art of *pandan* and *mengkuang* (types of screw-pine) plaiting. These are usually used to make plaited mats in bold and bright colours bearing attractive geometric designs or local flower and fruit motifs. Wood carving is another local craft which demonstrates the skill and dexterity of local craftsmen. Designs with motifs such as the *awan larat* (continuous floating clouds), *sulur kacang* (bean shoots), *daun ketola* (pumpkin leaves) and *bunga ketumbit* (the flower of a herb, *Leucas zeylanica*) are among the popular forms used by local wood carvers. Ornate carved wall panels, archways and partitions found in some of the traditional houses and royal palaces in Malaysia bear testimony to the superior quality of this particular craft.

Silver- and goldsmiths also play a significant role in producing some of the most magnificent craftwork Malaysia has ever known. High-quality silver and gold jewellery and other ornaments — like decorative tobacco boxes, belt buckles, dishes and plates, trinkets, bracelets, tea sets, hilts and sheaths of the kris and betel sets — are among the pride and joy of Malaysians.

Craftwork is an invaluable part of Malaysia's heritage, embodying the heart and soul of its people. It symbolises their sensitive thought, feeling and creativity, and is a medium in which public ethos, sensibility and aesthetic life have found full and secure expression.

The publication of this book on the handicrafts of Malaysia is an attempt to introduce Malaysian society by portraying its keen sensibility and its affinity with the natural environment, qualities that serve as the vehicle for its creative expression.

Dato' Haji Sulaiman Othman

EARTH

The earth's crust was formed millions of years ago through the primordial process of fire. The violent actions of volcanic eruptions thrust boiling magma to the earth's surface to form granite chains of hills and mountains, and the distinctive topographical features of the earth.

The hills and mountains were transformed with the passage of time. The action of hot gases of carbon dioxide, boron and fluorine decomposed the granite into feldspar, a mineral. Further weathering, or hydrolization, broke down the feldspar into silica, alumina and an alkali carbonate which was soluble and easily washed away by rain. The alumina and silica, combined with water, forms kaolinite or clay.

Clay can be categorised as primary or residual, or as secondary or sedimentary. The first group comprises non-plastic clays, found where they first formed, while secondary or sedimentary clays, through weathering by wind, rain and ice, are carried by streams and rivers towards the sea to settle in valleys and plains as layers of fine deposits, miles away from their source of origin.

Primary clays, known as kaolinite and with a chemical formula of $Al2O3. 2SiO_2.2H_2O$, are usually free of contaminants such as iron and give a clay cast which is white. They withstand high temperatures and are used to make porcelain ceramics. Other uses include the manufacture of floor and wall tiles, sanitary ware and tableware. Huge deposits are found in the Bidor area in Peninsular Malaysia and they are processed for domestic consumption or for export.

Secondary or sedimentary clays are lined with impurities. The verdant and luxurious Malaysian rainforests exude decomposed organic liquor into streams, giving most secondary clay deposits distinctive colours of buff-brown to grey and black, but this organic material is burnt off when the clay is fired. The lateritic content of Malaysian soil discolours clays from pink to iron-rust red when fired, because of the fine iron particles collected and mixed with the clay on its journey downstream. These clays are more plastic than the primary clays and are used in Malaysia's potteries and ceramic industries, from brick making to the manufacture of products like floor tiles, sanitary ware, tableware and fine ceramics.

In Peninsular Malaysia and in Sarawak and Sabah, there is an abundant supply of these plastic clays. They withstand high temperatures, an asset because it minimises the likelihood of their collapsing in high heat. Potters classify clays according to the temperatures they can be fired to without collapsing. Fireclays form the foundation of much of the soil in this country, and for that matter of the earth — the subsoil — itself, on which the primeval forests grew. Fireclays fire to 1,500° Celsius. Stoneware clay fires to 1,300° Celsius, ballclay — a very plastic clay — to 1,300° Celsius and earthenware to 1,100° Celsius. Some earthenware clays collapse even at 1,000° Celsius. Much of the traditional pottery of the Malays, Indians and Iban are of a low-fired category of clay known as terracotta clay.

Most clays cannot be dug up and used directly. The potter must compose his clay body from different clays and raw ingredients to achieve the properties desired for the types of wares he makes. The hardness of the clay, as well as its texture and colour, have to be taken into account for each pottery type. Pottery made in Malaysia is generally of the low-fired buff-brown and reddish terracotta clay of traditional potteries, or the high-fired stoneware clay used for the heavy clay products fired in dragon kilns. Porcelain is a recent development in this country.

NEOLITHIC POTTERY AND HISTORICAL PERSPECTIVES

The making of pottery is as old as mankind's history on earth. When Neolithic cave dwellers began to shift from a hunting lifestyle to an agricultural one, around 2,500 BC, the food-gathering people of prehistoric Malaysia began to develop vessels necessary to store grain and carry liquids. At around the same time, they began to make pottery for rituals and a developing belief system, especially afterlife beliefs, in relation to their perceptions of nature and the environment.

The discovery of the usefulness of clay is without doubt man's first great innovation in terms of artistry and science. Clay was found to be a malleable material that could be shaped with the fingers and hands to stay in a stable form on drying, and which could be made more permanent through the application of heat. Clay is essentially an organic material but when shaped into vessels and fired it becomes inorganic, and therefore non-perishable. Pottery, then, provides a fascinating basis for the study of the material culture of man's history on earth.

The abundance of potsherds excavated at different cave sites at Gua Musang, Gua Menteri and Gua Cha in Kelantan, at Bukit Tengku Lembu in Perlis, Bukit Kaplu at Kodiang in Kedah, Lenggong in Perak, Gua Bama and an open site at Nyong at the Tembeling in Pahang, suggests a phase of active pottery-making in this part of the world. Vessels found show a sense of symmetry and proportion and an understanding of function, both in the form produced and in the deployment of decorative elements.

Clay, when soft or at the leather-hard stage, presents a suitable surface for impressions of different kinds. Many of the earliest vessels have cord-marked impressions derived from a cord-wrapped beater or created with a cylindrical tool wound with string. The predominant cordmarking serves to prevent slippage when handled. Simple, incised wavy patterns using pointed instruments are also found on some of the vessels. A few have their surfaces burnished to a smooth polish. Some show a red surface, suggesting that a coating of slip was applied; it was probably derived from river silt with high iron content found in the area. The surface was probably burnished smooth with a pebble. This technique is still carried out by potters at Sayong in Perak, as well as at other traditional sites.

Neolithic pottery has a black surface because it is baked in a smouldering fire which coats the ware with soot and carbon. In a blazing fire, where there is plenty of oxygen in the gases around the fire, the natural colour of the clay is retained.

Vessels are mostly pinch-and-coiled and paddled. It is probable that round-bottomed pots were made with a round stone held inside while the bottom was paddled, much like the paddle-and-anvil method used in primitive potteries found in many parts of the world. The wheel was not used as the main tool, though a form of turntable made of wood could have been used to help make circular shapes. Simple dishes and bowls were made in one piece and footed vessels were built in stages.

Neolithic pottery was characterised, firstly, by a set of vessels associated with cooking; these were globular bowls with wide mouths. Next came a vessel with a bottom flattened for stability purposes, which was used for storing fruit or grain. Then devices for supports were made, and the perforated vessels found at Gua Musang and Tengku Lembu could represent the pot stands used for

A RARE HAND-COLOURED LITHOGRAPH AFTER A DRAWING BY D. E. SAINSON FROM *VOYAGE DE LA CORVETTE L'ASTROLABE EXECUTE PAR ORDRE DU ROI, PENDANT LES ANNEE 1826-29 SOUS LE COMMANDMENT DE MJ DUMONT D'URVILLE*, PUBLISHED IN PARIS AND EDITED BY J. TASLU IN 1835.

round-bottomed pots. A later development of the stand-like vessel was the carinated or keeled pot with a wide mouth, and finally, large storage vessels with flat bottoms and straight walls.

The abundance of potsherds found at Gua Musang suggests that caves were used for religious ceremonies by Neolithic people. Tweedy offers an explanation that "offerings of food were brought in vessels which were frequently broken, the fragments being stamped into the floor". And while the evidence of burnt kiln stands could indicate that caves were used as potteries for making and firing pots because of the shelter provided from rainstorms, the fact that "rock-shelters were used as burial grounds is certain, as both Noone (1939) and Williams Hunt (1952) record burials accompanied by grave furniture of entire pottery vessels and stone tools".

PATHWAYS, TRADE AND GOLD

Malaysia's main rivers are the pathways connecting the various regions of the country. The sites of Neolithic culture in Malaysia suggest that these passageways through the interior jungles of the Peninsula have been used for a very long time.

Successive waves of people coming to Malaysia used this network of inland routes to crisscross the country from east to west, or vice versa. The presence of gold in auriferous mines in Kelantan and Pahang may have been what stimulated traders from hemispheres to the north-east and the west of the Malayan Peninsula to vie for the trading of gold, aromatics and other exotic goods.

In the historical account of Malaysia, the period before the development of the Malay sultanates which spread from Melaka in the 15th century AD is still obscure, and the data scanty. Records of Chinese chroniclers suggest — according to Anker Rentse and based on the publications of Dato' Roland Braddell, J. L. Moens and Quadrich-Wales — that an earlier Malay civilisation could have been established on the East Coast, in the north-eastern state of Kelantan (probably the *Ho-lo-tan* of the Chinese chroniclers of the early Sung period). Important settlements of traders were found from about 1st to 10th centuries AD and influences from the north, north-east and west could well have left their impressions upon the early era of Malay culture.

The Kelantan River was open to Malay shipping 300 km upstream, and pathways connect the tributaries to the borders of Perak and Pahang. One route west connects the upper reaches of the Patani River in Thailand through the Sungei Telubin and the Pergau, a tributary of the Kelantan River, to Kuala Merbok in Kedah, passing through the present Sungei Patani. Another route runs southwardly to the Sai, a tributary of the Tembeling, and then to the Jelai in Ulu Pahang, eventually connecting to Melaka. (Anker Rentse, "A Historical Note on the Northeastern States," *JMBRAS* vol. 20 (1) 1947). The connection can only be conjectured, but it is fascinating to point out that many traditional Malay pottery sites are found on or near these ancient routes — for instance the Kampung Mambong pottery on the Kelantan River above Kuala Krai, the Alor Merah and Sungei Dua sites in Kedah, the Bukit Gantang, Sayong and Pulau Tiga potteries on the Perak River, and the Pasir Durian pottery on the River Tembeling in Pahang.

MALAY POTTERY

An account of Malay pottery in Perak by Leonard Wray (*Journal of the Anthropological Institute of Great Britain and Ireland.*, vol. 33, 1903) pointed out "the great antiquity of the art, and ... the certainty of its having come down to the present time without influence from the more civilised nations who have, from time to time, imparted new arts and ideas to the Malayan inhabitants of the peninsula". He was referring to the potter's wheel used in India and China from a very remote period, which has never been known to the Malays. "Malayan pottery may be looked upon as a survival... of a phase in the ceramic art far anterior to that to be found in other countries in a similar state of advancement."

No Malay pottery older than 250 years has been found, however. The gap between the pottery of prehistory and that of the Malays of the past 200 years is intriguing and will remain unclear until further research brings light to this obscure phase. One reason for the lack of evidence could be the very fragile nature of Malay pottery. The corrosive action of the soil and the humid conditions of an equatorial climate could be other reasons why no traces of the art are left to us. The trade of goods from Persia, India and China — which went on for much of this period — included ceramic ware of greater durability and sophistication and this could have been preferred to the less durable Malay pottery. Carried out on a very small scale, for home use mostly, it may not have survived the import of more attractive wares.

Malay pottery is traditionally the domain of women, and the craft is carried out as a leisure or incidental occupation when there is time between household and other domestic chores, or during the relatively inactive period between the rice-growing seasons. The women making pottery in the traditional way today are elderly women. At Mambong or in the Tembeling, the women are in their sixties. Their sensitivity to form is abundantly shown by the variety of shapes produced. Pottery forms are gracefully proportioned and the decorations exquisite and subtle.

POTTERY TYPES AND SHAPES

Four main types of Malay pottery can be identified. The first type is the water container called a *buyung*. It is generally large and has a wide body. The side rises from the wide belly at an incline to a short cylindrical neck, ending at the mouth with an everted lip. It is similar in shape to the Indian brassware water container which is widely distributed in Asia, and is a shape that has been made for a very long time. Early trading of Indian goods could have brought this form to Malay pottery. The Indian potteries at Parit Buntar and Kuala Selangor still make an identical form to this day. A smaller version, also for carrying water, is called the *geluk*. This vessel has a globular body and a straight or flared neck, with a well-defined lip. The bulbous body usually has raised relief ribs vertically or diagonally arranged round the pot, a form derived from the fruit of the *assam glugor* tree, which is common to riverine kampungs.

The second type of Malay pottery is called the *belanga*. It is a wide-rimmed pot with a rounded bottom, usually with slightly inclined sides. The lip is thick and firm to provide stability in handling. It is a pot used for cooking and is claimed by housewives to be the most suitable vessel for curries. Like the round-bottomed *wok*, heat is distributed more evenly round the pot. The open body of the clay used

allows for thermal shocks when the pot is placed over a gas flame. It will not crack like pots made of a denser and seemingly stronger clay body. The *belanga* type produced at the Tembeling pottery is rounder and larger and has a shape reminiscent of Neolithic pottery. The form could have been handed down through generations of potters. A pot similar in shape and generally used for cooking is called a *periok*, though smaller in size. Those produced at Mambong are reddish-brown because of the high content of iron in the clay. They have more rounded bodies and come with covers which have dotted impressions arranged round the knobs. This kind of knob is commonly found on covers of brassware vessels. Mambong pottery has a unique organic character of its own.

A third distinctive type of Malay pottery, though invariably called *periok*, is the carinated vessel-form produced exclusively at Tembeling. It is the *terenang* and ranges from a light ochre to dark red-brown. Traditionally used for carrying water, it has a special use as a vessel for keeping holy water to cure the sick. The *terenang* is angular in form and decorated with carved serrated designs at the lip and edges, where a change in plane occurs drastically as the pot rises from its foot. The shoulder and neck are stamped with geometrical motifs. Others have elaborately carved tendril designs. The *terenang* is identical in form to brassware vessels which were once made to a fair extent in Kelantan. Now these brassware vessels are done mostly in Terengganu, where the craft survives to this day at Ladang and Tanjung in Kuala Terengganu. The Perak Museum in Taiping and the Sultan Abu Bakar Museum in Pekan have a fine collection of these unique *terenang*.

Then comes the fourth range of Malay pottery, the ubiquitous gourd-shaped water bottles called *labu*. These are inspired by the bottle-gourd (*Lagennaria vulgaris, ser.*) and coconut shell forms. Different names are given depending on variations in form. An exact copy of the bottle-gourd is called *labu tanah*, literally earth gourd. A well-defined footed one is called *labu kaki*. One with a straight cylindrical neck is called *labu pucung*. *Pucung* is a grey heron (*ardea cinerea*) found in paddy fields. A water bottle with a series of distended bulges around the body is called *labu glugor*, named after the as*sam glugor*. A *labu* with raised ribbings of clay arranged vertically or diagonally around the body is known as *labu panai*.

A similar form that has a pouring spout is the kendi, an ancient form found in many countries, from Japan to the Middle East. When held by the neck, which is usually long, and poured through the spout, a steady stream flows out and can be directed to the mouth, doing away with the need for drinking cups. This kendi form, like those derived from the bottle-gourd, is usually made of a low temperature terracotta clay with a honeycombed, porous body. It is usually found with a coating of damar-resin at the bottom. This is in order to prevent water from oozing out from below. The main body of the pot sweats and perspires in the evaporation process, and the water contained inside is cooled, making it a very useful water bottle.

A few other types of pottery are also produced and these are the incense burners called *perasapan*, widely used for religious and ceremonial purposes, and the *kukusan*, which is a steamer used for steaming glutinous rice (*pulut*). Vases, piggybanks and ashtrays simulating fruits and other forms derived from the kampung environment are recent introductions.

DECORATION

A plethora of motifs and patterns with romantic names are applied in Malay pottery. Motifs are derived from nature, especially the exotic flora of a verdant rainforest, background to life in the Peninsula with its myriad shapes, textures and patterns. Decorations reveal motifs and patterns stylised from flowers such as the *bunga cengkih* (aromatic clove), *bunga padi, bunga tanjung, bunga lawang* and so on. Bamboo shoots are given the name *pucuk rebung*. Other names abound for a variety of motifs abstracted and stylised from the flora and fauna of a luxuriant jungle. Even basic geometric patterns are related to nature, like the hatched pattern referred to as *bunga cakar ayam* or fowl-scratched pattern.

Most motifs are carved on the ends of small pieces of wood and used as stamps. Other apparatus include bamboo strips with serrated edges used to create dotted linear patterns. Sharp pointed instruments are used for making incisions and thinly sliced strips of bamboo are used for scraping and cutting. String and band patterns are stamped around pots and vessels, giving a unique rhythm harmonised with form. When subtly executed, they exhibit the best in Malay pottery.

BUILDING AND FIRING TECHNIQUES

The clay used for Malay pottery is a terracotta clay found by streams, riverbanks and paddy fields. That found near anthills is preferred because of its great plasticity. Clay for the Sayong and Pulau Tiga potteries once came from Temong upriver (Wray). Other clays from the district are now used and they vary in colour from black to ochery brown or buff-white. The Malay potters at Mambong, Kuala Krai get theirs from a clay pit they say never depletes but constantly replenishes itself. In the old days, taboos or *pantang larang* were associated with digging for clay. Different areas have their specific taboos. One general one is that menstruating women are not allowed in the vicinity when clay is being dug up. The clay is usually mixed with fine sand and pounded in a foot-pounder called a *lesong kaki,* after which it is sieved. It is mixed with water and kneaded to a plastic consistency. The fine sand opens out the clay body, providing pores for the clay to 'breathe'.

As Wray had noticed nearly a hundred years ago when he was Director of the Taiping Museum, the potter's wheel was unknown to Malay potters. The wheel seen at pottery sites today is a recent phenomenon. Elderly Malay women are still making pottery the traditional way, by hand. The pinch-and-coil method, common to most primitive pottery, is used. A wooden dish or plate acts as a base or turntable. Wooden paddles, some with carved patterns, as well as other very simple homemade tools of bamboo or wood, are used. The purpose of the carved wooden paddles — used to beat the pot — is to shape the pot and thin its walls, rather than primarily to leave an impression, as with Neolithic, Iban or Thai pottery. Some pots are formed in one piece while others are built in stages, depending on the type being made. They are then left to dry. At the leather-hard stage, the surface is given a good rubover with smooth pebbles. This rubbing, called burnishing, produces a smooth surface and results in the kind of polished sheen seen in Malay pottery. Slightly different methods of firing are used in the different pottery sites. At Sayong, pots are placed inverted on a rack made from branches of trees, with a fire pit

A *PERIOK* WITH HANDLES AND COVER MADE AT KAMPUNG MAMBONG IN KUALA KRAI IN KELANTAN. THE FORM RESEMBLES A BRASSWARE VESSEL WHICH HAS A SIMILAR KNOB ON THE COVER. THE IMPRESSED DECORATIONS ARE ACHIEVED WITH STRIPS OF BAMBOO.

below. After four to five hours, the pots are taken off and put into the glowing embers of the fire pit. The rack is removed and the big fire stoked with dry bamboo splits. After about an hour's firing, the pots are removed from the embers with a pole and buried in rice chaff. The reducing condition blackens the pots. Others are taken out to cool to retain the natural colour of the earthy clay. The colour can be from yellowish brown through grey to rust-red, depending on the iron content.

This blackening of the surface by a reducing condition — when the pot smoulders in dry combustible materials like rice husk — is the outcome of the same basic natural process that gives us smoke and fire. Different shades of black, from light grey to metallic black, give the material a beauty and textural quality that requires no other superfluous decoration. It is achieved by this process alone. Black paint or wax cannot impart the same property; rather, they can be antithetical to the aesthetics of a fine tradition. Paint is a dead material and it jars the senses. Decorative effects of overly high relief or sprigged floral designs can be too insistent and distracting as well.

Glazed pottery is another dimension altogether of the potter's art. Glaze was unknown to Malay potters until introduced in recent years. The cultural origins of Malay pottery — without the use of glaze technologies like those achieved in China — is quintessentially Malay. By achieving so much, creating such a wide range of pottery types and shapes with simple earthy materials and simple tools, Malay pottery can hold its own when compared to pottery from other parts of the world. What is more, it is endorsed by tradition. The organic relationship between potter and user is sympathetically established and plays an important symbolic role. The combination of decorative elements derived organically from nature, together with abstract geometric designs, are inherent in the Malay cultural heritage. Another aspect is craftsmanship, which is of paramount importance in the execution of the handicraft being made. Anything resembling poor craftsmanship is frowned upon.

The families of Puan Hamid and Puan Zam are typical families at Kampung Kepala Bendang of Sayong, carrying on a tradition of pottery-making handed down from generations of potters. Husband En. Zam helps at the training centre at Enggor while En. Hamid is an expert in the herbal medicinal properties of jungle roots. Puan Hasnah, a descendant of a respected family of potters, is now very old, and ill health has prevented her from making any more pottery for some time now. However, the tradition lives on, passed down to younger generations of potters. Malay potteries are being developed not only at traditional sites but also elsewhere in the country, as a result of the training programmes and support systems provided by the Malaysian Handicraft Development Corporation. Co-operatives are set up wherever possible and the ones at Sayong are particularly well-established. Through these ventures new equipment, such as gas kilns and electric wheels, and plaster-mould production techniques have been introduced. At Sayong, the new technology works side by side with traditional methods.

A new range of pottery is emerging from these co-operative ventures. A wide variety of shapes are being produced, particularly for the consumer market. They come in various sizes, many still retaining the impressed decoration of traditional pottery. On-glaze enamel decorations of Malaysian flowers are beginning to appear as well. The crucial problem confronting the craft is the conflict of tradition, on the

one hand, and the economics of pottery production for profit on the other. New production technologies have the power as well as the limitation to reduce the craft to mere tourist commodities — aesthetically empty, and spiritually and culturally insignificant. Plaster-mould production technology can multiply an invidious form by the hundreds, and their proliferation can dull our senses. Whether, and how, time-tested traditions reflect meaning and cultural identity are questions which only time and aesthetic sensitivity can decide. Education and the right philosophical approach within a cultural framework will help carry the tradition in good form into the future.

INDIAN POTTERY

There are two Indian pottery centres where low-fired terracotta ware of South Indian origin is made. One is situated at Kampung Kedah in Parit Buntar, a few kilometres north of Bagan Serai, on the road to Butterworth, and the other at Batu Dua, Jalan Kelang, just south of Kuala Selangor. These potteries produce vessel forms handed down from generations. Some statuary is also produced for temple and religious purposes. Pottery vessels are needed for many occasions — marriages, death rites, blessings for temples, the festival of lights, blessings to God Ganesh, the harvest festival and so on.

In 1850 Marimuthu Velar, a potter from South India, migrated to the Peninsula and set up the Devaraj pottery at Kampung Kedah in Parit Buntar. His son Kandasamy, having learnt the craft from a young age, continued with it when the old man passed on. His two sons, Loga and Parama, now in their thirties, are carrying on the tradition. Another South Indian, M. Vengadasalam, came to Malaysia seventy-two years ago, and worked as a rubber tapper in Gemas. Having come from a family of potters, he set up a pottery at Kuala Selangor after the war. His son Ramadas runs the pottery now with his wife.

In order to prevent his forebears' tradition of pottery-making from fading away after his years of toil, Ramadas has created two branch potteries, one managed by his sister Sellama and the other by his adopted son, Murugan. Loga Velar in Kampung Kedah, on the other hand, is seeing to it that his children will not follow in his footsteps. Eking out a livelihood as a potter will not be for them. He feels the conditions are too shackling and the profits demeaningly low. He is determined to see that his children receive an education that will allow them to free themselves from the fate he was destined to.

A limited range of vessel forms is produced in these potteries. One is a cooking pot with a wide mouth, commonly known by the Malay name *belanga* or *periok*. Another pot similar in shape to a *buyung* is for cooking rice and is made in different sizes. Indian pottery is never over-decorated, the ornamentation being limited to a simple stamped dot design running round the shoulder of the pot. Another item made is the oil burner, which is a small dish pinched at the rim to keep the wick in place. It is used in temples or at religious ceremonies and festivals. The incense burner is a perforated dish fixed to a foot and provided with a handle and used in religious rituals and other ceremonial occasions. Indian pottery is usually brushed with an iron red slip to give the reddish colour preferred by customers.

The Indian potteries are sited near coastal areas where a pulpy and brackish clay is found. Sand is mixed to it to produce a low temperature open clay body. The wheel has been known to Indian potters

FACING PAGE: EXAMPLES OF TWO TYPES OF MALAY POTTERY. TOP: WATER CONTAINERS WITH SPOUTS, DERIVED IN FORM FROM AN ANCIENT BOTTLE CALLED THE KENDI. IT HAS A LONG NECK WHICH CAN BE GRASPED FIRMLY BY THE HAND, ENABLING THE WATER FROM THE SPOUT TO BE DIRECTED TO THE MOUTH, MAKING THE USE OF CUPS UNNECESSARY. BOTTOM: WIDE-BELLIED POTS CALLED *BUYUNG*, USED FOR CARRYING WATER AND REMINISCENT OF BRASSWARE WATER CONTAINERS OF INDIAN ORIGIN. COLOUR VARIATIONS ARE DUE TO THE DIFFERENT CONTENT OF IRON PARTICLES IN THE CLAY. THE MORE THE IRON, THE MORE RUST-RED THE POT.

for most of their long historical tradition. A large wooden wheel not unlike a bullock-cart wheel, balanced by a metal pin in the centre, was once used. A helper was needed to spin the wheel, using a pole inserted into a hole on the rim. The wheel's weight provided the momentum and the potter could throw a pot after a number of spins. Today, wheels are fabricated from motor parts. The drive is provided by an electric motor and speed is controlled by the gear shift-stick (usually sawn off to a stump) and manipulated by the toes. The potter can pull off a number of pots from a hump of clay on such a wheel.

Indian pots are thrown on the wheel without a bottom and then allowed to dry. The potter sits on the floor with his feet pulled in and the leather-hard pot placed snugly on the sole of one foot. A rounded cement form acting as an anvil is held on the inside. The open base of the pot is closed by repeatedly beating from the wall towards the centre with a beater as the pot is turned round. This paddle-and-anvil method is characteristic of Indian pottery. Glaze is never used by Indian potters in this country. When the pots are dry, they are fired in an open space. This involves inverting the pots over a pile of dry brushwood, coconut shells and husks. Thicker pieces of wood and branches cover the pile, over which *lallang* grass is plastered with mud to form a conical mound. The bottom rim and top end are left uncovered. A fire is set to the bottom rim round the pile and a strong fire builds up within. The top end, uncovered by slip, acts as a chimney for gases to spill out. An hour's firing will reduce all combustible material to ashes. A wood-fire type of kiln is now used. Plaster moulds help to increase production. New clay bodies have been introduced unwittingly, good for a certain range of pottery but disastrous for the curry pot, which is usually made of low temperature terracotta clay.

CHINESE DRAGON KILN POTTERY

Situated in the west coast countryside of Peninsular Malaysia are the long dragon kilns of the Chinese potters, measuring 18 to 45m long. They are always roofed with corrugated iron from the fire mouths to the chimney ends. They are usually sited around clay deposits. Similar kilns are found on the outskirts of Kuching and Sibu in Sarawak and Kota Kinabalu in Sabah. These are kilns introduced over a hundred years ago by immigrant Chinese, mostly Teochews (Chaozhou) from Swatow (Shantou) in Guangdong Province. They are built on gentle slopes. Internal dimensions at the widest end can be two metres high and two metres wide. A 45m-long kiln can accommodate a fair amount of pottery. The rubber plantations of Peninsular Malaysia created a vast new demand at the turn of the century for rubber cups, small vessels to hold the latex running down the cuts of trees. Families of potters from Swatow came to set up potteries in areas where good deposits of clay could be found. We find clusters of these dragon kilns established at the Kuala Kangsar Road area north of Ipoh because of the good clay found, with a river flowing nearby to supply the water needed. Another cluster of kilns was set up in the Segambut area of Kuala Lumpur. Elsewhere, from Kedah to Johor, these kilns were built around clay deposits.

One of the oldest potteries in the Kuala Kangsar Road area is the Toh Seng Heng Pottery. Descendants and relatives of the original ten families who set up potteries here have spread out to establish potteries in Sungei Siput, Batu Gajah, Gopeng and Beruas. There are fifty potteries now in the district north of Ipoh, with no less than eighty dragon kilns, and they provide employment to over 1,800 people. Fourth generation descendants of the original ten families are now actively involved in making flower pots and *kong-jars* for the world market. Container loads of colourfully glazed stoneware flower pots and jars are exported to the United States, Australia, Europe and the United Kingdom.

The Segambut potteries in the Kuala Lumpur area are almost all gone now, evicted for the development of housing estates and new factories. Pressure to move comes partly because of the pollution spewed out from wood-fired kilns. Still, scrubbers can be installed to clean the polluting discharge, and indeed this is being done to kilns in the Ipoh district. The oldest surviving pottery in Segambut is the Goh Ban Huat Pottery, now a modern factory producing high-end tableware and sanitary ware.

The dragon kiln potteries produce mainly stoneware flower pots and water jars. Other clay products include joss stick holders, rubber cups, drainpipes, clay stoves and specially designed items. A jigging machine, a uniquely local invention, turns out huge quantities of flower pots and jars for the domestic as well as export markets. The huge *kong-jars* are partly thrown on the wheel and partly built up with thick coils of clay. They are then beaten with wooden paddles and refined on the wheel.

Clay used for these wares is a composition of ballclay and sandy clay mixed and extruded through a pug mill. It is a durable stoneware body, and the normal temperature products are fired to is1,240° Celsius. Glaze is a recipe of marine clay or sea mud and lime. The sea mud comes from the mudflats at Port Klang in Selangor. Under a reducing condition of firing, the glaze is greenish in colour. Oxidised firing produces a golden honey glaze. Salt glazing is also done. Coarse rock salt is fed through the side stoke holes when a particular section has reached the right temperature. The salt vaporises in the kiln chamber and forms a film on the surface of the pot. When combined with the silica, the salt acts as a flux and a melt is produced to give a salt glaze to the surface of the pot. A greenish runny glaze is formed in the salt atmosphere when pots are glazed with the sea mud-lime composition.

A TYPICAL LOW-FIRED GLOBULAR POT FROM SARAWAK MADE BY IBAN POTTERS. THE OVERALL RELIEF PATTERN WAS THE RESULT OF IMPRESSIONS CREATED BY THE CARVED WOODEN BEATER THE POTTER USED WHEN PADDLING TO FORM THE POT.

SARAWAK POTTERY

Pottery made in Sarawak is of two distinctive types, one done by the Iban, Murut and Kelabit potters and the other, like in Peninsular Malaysia, by Chinese potters from Swatow. The pottery of the various Dayak peoples is done by women and it is much like the simple low-fired pottery done throughout the world. It is hand moulded, and the common paddle-and-anvil method is used. Pottery is made for utilitarian purposes, though sometimes vessels made are used in Iban ceremonies connected with dye-mixing for weaving *pua*. Iban pottery closely resembles the Neolithic pottery found in archeological excavations in Sarawak, and may be a tradition handed down from the remote past. The method of preparing the clay is similar to that used in Malay pottery. Clay is obtained from river banks, then dried and refined by sieving. It is mixed with water, kneaded and pounded until a plastic state is achieved. Sometimes bran, fine rice chaff or ground powder from discarded pots (grog) is mixed with the clay. The globular form of Iban pottery is achieved by pressing a round stone into a lump of clay. The lump is supported on the lap of the potter and beaten repeatedly with a paddle carved with diagonal or crossed lines. The form swells into a pot as the lump of clay is beaten and turned round and round. The paddle leaves impressions all over the pot, creating a textural quality and beauty achieved by the simple and spontaneous process of making it. No other decoration is necessary. Iban pottery is never decorated with incised designs.

Firing is similar to the open fire of primitive pottery. Fired pots are porous. With constant use a layer of grease and soot is deposited, making them watertight. Sometimes hot pots are soaked in a brew made of mangrove bark and water called *samak*, or they are coated with damar-resin, like the Malay labu pots. Nowadays factory-made ceramics and enamel wares are easily available, and if the craft is still practised at all, it may be carried out in very remote longhouses.

The Chinese potters on the outskirts of Kuching and Sibu produce stoneware jars decorated with dragon designs, like their forefathers used to do in China. They are similar to the jars exported to Southeast Asian countries from the 12th century onwards. These jars are highly prized by the Iban and are collected for storage purposes. They are especially good for bringing perishable goods upriver to longhouses in the interior. They are also coveted as heirlooms and status symbols by the longhouses. The number of jars a man possesses is synonymous with his wealth and social standing in the community. Another type of pottery produced in large quantities for the tourist market is the tall vase. It comes in a form not unlike the *labu* shape, although with a less bulbous body. It has a firm foot and a tall, straight cylindrical neck with a large everted lip. It is highly decorated with Dayak designs, either carved through the enamel glaze or brushed on with black, brown and blue enamel colours as on-glaze decoration. Other kinds of pottery produced include flower pots, rubber cups, basins and jars which are similar to those made by ancestors in China long ago.

CONCLUSION

The present century has been perceived as a period of dramatic change. Inventions and ideas of this century appear to equal or overwhelm the sum total of all the progress of past centuries. The speed of the information revolution and the new technologies that have swept into our lives from the 1950's onwards have propelled us on, leaving us with little time to contemplate these changes.

In the field of ceramics, as in all areas of creative activity, potters have been challenged to explore new ways of doing things. Tradition inevitably comes into conflict with economics; aesthetics with commercialism. Traditional ways of doing things have to be re-examined and new forms need to be explored. The craft of pottery, like all other crafts of tradition, will be subjected to the changes happening in this country. Opportunities created will provide craftsmen with the freedom to explore. Aesthetic sensibilities for cultural traditions and sensitive perceptions of new and meaningful directions in form are issues that need to be tackled as Malaysian potters move into the future.

Yeoh Jin Leng

FACING PAGE:
EXAMPLES OF GOURD-
SHAPED WATER BOTTLES
CALLED *LABU*. THE VESSEL
ON THE EXTREME RIGHT
IS MORE OR LESS AN
IDENTICAL FORM OF A
BOTTLE-GOURD AND IS
GIVEN THE NAME *LABU
TANAH*, LITERALLY EARTH
GOURD. FOOTED ONES
ARE KNOWN AS *LABU
KAKI*. THOSE WITH
RAISED RIBS OF CLAY
ROUND THE BODY ARE
CALLED *LABU PANAI*
SOME ARE OVERLY
CARVED, GIVING THE
FEELING THAT THEY ARE
MADE OF WOOD, LIKE
THE POT ON THE LEFT.
THE BLACK *LABU PANAI* IN
THE BACKGROUND IS
MOUNTED WITH SILVER
TO SERVE AS A LIP.
BELOW: A CARINATED
VESSEL FORM CALLED A
TERENANG. THIS FORM IS
CHARACTERISTIC OF THE
TYPE OF POTTERY ONCE
MADE AT TEMBELING IN
PAHANG. IT IS USED FOR
KEEPING HOLY WATER
TO CURE THE SICK.

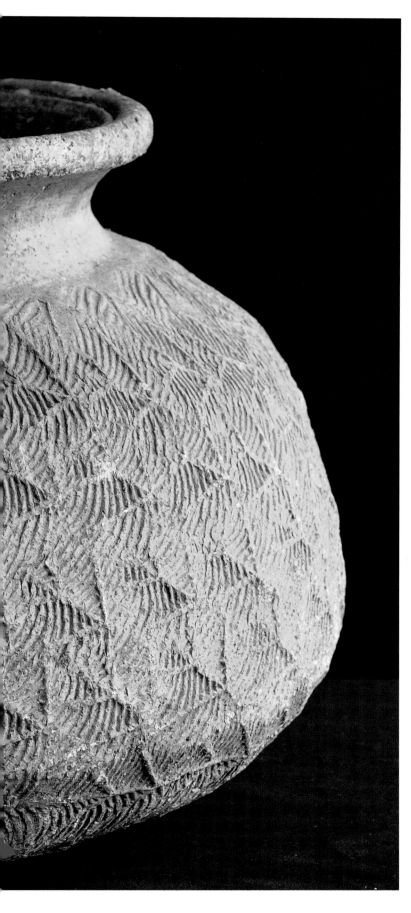

LEFT: THIS GLOBULAR
POT WITH IMPRESSED
DECORATIONS IS FROM
THE TERENGGANU
MUSEUM. SUCH
DECORATIONS WERE
IMPRESSED INTO THE
CLAY WITH A CARVED
WOODEN STAMP WHILE
THE CLAY WAS STILL
SOFT. POTS WITH
SIMILAR DECORATIONS
HAVE ALSO BEEN FOUND
IN KELANTAN.
RIGHT: AN IBAN POT
DECORATED THROUGH
THE PADDLE-AND-
ANVIL METHOD.

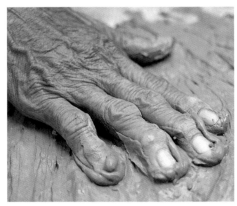

THIS PAGE, TOP TO
BOTTOM: PLASTIC CLAY
USUALLY FOUND IN
ALLUVIAL PLAINS OR BY
THE BANKS OF RIVERS IS
DRIED IN THE SUN, THEN
MIXED WITH FINE SIFTED
RIVER SAND TO OPEN
OUT THE CLAY BODY.
WATER IS ADDED AND
THE MIXTURE KNEADED
TO TURN IT INTO PLASTIC
CLAY READY FOR USE.
FACING PAGE: THE POT
ON THE TURNING WHEEL
IS BEING CARVED WITH
GROOVED LINES USING
A RESHAPED HACKSAW
BLADE. THE RINGS ROUND
THE POT ACT AS
GUIDELINES FOR THE
STAMPED DECORATIONS
THE POTTER WILL ETCH
ON THE POT TO
CREATE THE BEAUTIFUL
PATTERNS FOUND IN
MALAY POTTERY.

FACING PAGE: A POT
BEING THROWN ON THE
WHEEL. FINGERS AND
HANDS ARE USED IN
DIFFERENT WAYS TO GIVE
SHAPE AND FORM TO
THE PLASTIC CLAY.
THIS PAGE: A ROW OF
OIL LAMPS BEING MADE.
A SMALL ROUND DISH IS
FIRST THROWN OFF A
HUMP OF CLAY ON THE
WHEEL. THE RIM IS THEN
PINCHED TO HOLD THE
WICK. THESE OIL LAMPS
ARE USED FOR THE
INDIAN FESTIVAL OF
LIGHTS, AS WELL AS FOR
OTHER TEMPLE
CEREMONIES.

THIS RELIEF PLAQUE
OF KANNAN AND RATHA,
OF INDIAN MYTHOLOGY,
IS CAST IN CLAY.
IT WAS TAKEN OFF
A MOULD MADE OF
PLASTER-OF-PARIS, A
MATERIAL WHICH IS
EXTENSIVELY USED IN
THE MASS PRODUCTION
OF CERAMICS. HUNDREDS
OF IDENTICAL IMAGES
CAN BE PRODUCED
FROM MOULDS USING
THIS MATERIAL.

A POTTER STOKING
THE FIRE MOUTH OF
A KILN WITH WASTE
FIREWOOD. INDIAN
POTTERY WAS TRADI-
TIONALLY MADE USING
AN OPEN FIRE. A KILN LIKE
THIS ONE IS A RECENT
INTRODUCTION AND IS
AN UPDRAUGHT KILN.
HIGHER TEMPERATURES
CAN BE ACHIEVED
AND POTS ARE DENSER
AND MORE DURABLE.

FACING PAGE, TOP: A STACK OF FLOWER POTS MADE USING A JIGGER TYPE OF MACHINE, IN CHINESE DRAGON KILN POTTERIES FROM THE IPOH DISTRICT. A DRAGON KILN MAY BE UP TO 45M LONG, WITH INTERNAL DIMENSIONS OF TWO METRES HIGH AND TWO METRES WIDE. THESE DRAGON KILNS WERE FIRST INTRODUCED INTO THE COUNTRY TO MAKE THE RUBBER CUPS USED BY RUBBER PLANTATIONS. BOTTOM PICTURE SHOWS A DRAGON KILN BUTTRESSED WITH A THICK WALL OF BRICKS AS SUPPORT. A DOORWAY FOR LOADING POTS CAN BE SEEN IN THE MIDDLE. THIS PAGE: A KILN-CAR OF POTTERY IS PUSHED INTO A SHUTTLE KILN FOR FIRING. MORE INDUSTRIAL KILNS OF THIS TYPE ARE NOW BEING INTRODUCED TO MEET THE GROWING DEMAND FOR HIGH-END CERAMIC WARE.

FIBRES

Malaysia's natural environment allows man to co-exist — even thrive — with nature in a variety of habitats. Inter-relationships with plants and animals and the forest have existed for millennia, providing ways for different human communities to live in harmony in a variety of environments. Malaysia can still boast of very rich rainforests which provide food and material for forest and non-forest dwellers alike. Traditionally, the peoples who have used the forest — mainly indigenous peoples from the interiors of Sabah and Sarawak, although some tribes still exist on the West Coast in West Malaysia — have manufactured implements and produced crafts from this rich bank of natural resources. Malaysia's rainforests also provide considerable supplies of produce, especially hard wood timbers, which continue to make substantial contributions to state and national economies.

Not all of Malaysia's useful materials for craft making come from the jungle. Its sandy coasts also allow the growth of certain plants which are an important source of plant fibre for craft work. Its plains and other open spaces provide other raw materials. The local craftsperson uses whatever primary material can be collected from the immediate environment. The craft maker may have to improvise and trade or barter for required components that may be lacking in the vicinity, but in general objects made from plant fibre mirror the environment from where they originate.

Environmental controls are also integral to the cultures of many of the indigenous peoples who manufacture crafts. The environment is usually exploited only for what it can yield to fulfill an immediate need. Seldom, if ever, are the products extracted solely for surplus or for profit. Many of these societies, especially those still observing and maintaining traditional animistic beliefs, have a healthy respect for plants and animals. They believe that these have or are inhabited by spirits which must be placated, cajoled or even avoided before trees and plants can be harvested or removed. This belief also extends to the hunting of animals for food or for other purposes. To live in balance with nature, the lives of these indigenous peoples are governed and sanctioned by a series of taboos and ritual observances which protect their environment, and so protect them. For centuries these people have adapted to their environment and used its products without destroying the source. Many of these traditional beliefs also continue to be manifested in the motifs and forms of their arts and crafts, serving to remind them of their all-important relationship with nature.

However, population pressures, urbanisation and various economic and social philosophies of progress and development have, over the ages, invariably made incursions on these environments and have eroded the effectiveness of traditional beliefs of environmental protection. Fortunately, the Malaysian government has not been unaware of these incidences of environmental degradation. Traditional controls and official environmental conservation policies have generally ensured that large tracts of forests and other habitats are preserved and protected. These habitats continue to produce the resource materials required for the country's burgeoning craft manufacture — one which now serves mostly the growing tourist and export markets. Changes to landscapes and biological habitats are inevitable, but as long as the flora and fauna are sustainable and care is taken to avoid their over-exploitation, the long-term future of the botanical base of Malaysia's craft manufacture is assured.

PRECEDING PAGES: AN IBAN HARVESTING BASKET CALLED *SINTONG*, MADE FROM UNDYED RATTAN, USING THE TYPICAL INTRICATE HERRING-BONE TYPE PATTERN THAT IS A COMMON FEATURE OF IBAN BASKETRY.
FACING PAGE: MAN'S INTER-RELATIONSHIP WITH HIS ENVIRONMENT HAS ALLOWED HIM TO THRIVE IN HARMONY WITH NATURE FOR MILLENIA IN A VARIETY OF HABITATS. HE EXPLOITS HIS ENVIRON-MENT FOR FOOD, SHELTER AND RAW MATERIALS FOR CRAFT MANUFACTURE TO SERVE HIS IMMEDIATE NEEDS. THE OBJECTS THAT HE PRODUCES OFTEN MIRROR THE ENVIRON-MENT FROM WHERE THEY ORIGINATE.

OVERLAPPING TRADITIONS

The Dongson bronze age culture of the first millennium BC had its base in what is known today as Vietnam, and had spread by the 2nd century BC throughout Southeast Asia and into the Malay Archipelago. It introduced decorative art forms and motifs that enriched the otherwise simple indigenous arts and crafts of the period. Indeed, the motifs and designs of some of today's crafts are remnants of the Dongson culture. As Southeast Asia became integrated into the world trade network, cultural input from India and China increased, providing the basis for a long history of Indian and Chinese influence in Southeast Asia. Hindu and Buddhist empires arose in Southeast Asia, and extended their influence in the region. In Malaysia, Hindu and Buddhist traditions found their way into local customs. Islam, which came later, integrated with the resulting cultures, blending with existing traditions and giving new life to local art forms, or encouraging the development of new ones.

Sabah, Malaysia's easternmost state on the northern part of the island of Borneo, was generally bypassed in the sweep of Hindu and Buddhist influences. As sea-faring communities settled on the coasts of Borneo, many of Sabah's indigenous peoples moved inland, and remained isolated and insulated from the influences of these civilisations. Of all the external influences, Islam had the greatest impact on local material culture, especially among those communities found on the coasts and upper reaches of accessible rivers. This reflects the activities of Muslim traders who visited the neighbouring Philippines, as well as the growth and expansion of the Brunei empire on the northern coast of Borneo. The impenetrable jungle-covered interior of Borneo and its hostile tribes discouraged foreign colonisation and the settlement of much of the land and its interior. So, for centuries, the remote tribes of Sabah, and to some extent, Sarawak in the interior, remained free from the later incursions and invasions on the coasts. This history is strongly reflected in craft manufacturing traditions, which retain much of the old animistic motifs and anthropomorphic forms, and display a varied use of materials from the jungle.

ARTS AND CRAFTS

In the Malay Archipelago, very little distinction is made between fine arts and crafts. Both are interlinked. The Western sense of art as an independent aesthetic entity does not exist in the traditional context. The objects that people in this region — and the rest of Southeast Asia — fashion and create are based on function and utility, and are generally expressions of part of their lives. This is particularly true of objects made largely from plant material taken from the environment. Their purpose illustrates their meaning: most objects are to be used, symbols have an abstract quality, and utility is manifest in worship and veneration in religious rituals and practices.

The forms and styles of many types of baskets and similar objects are the result of thousands of years of development. The different materials used also reflect the extremely varied environments in which these objects are made. The countries of Southeast Asia share many elements of a common heritage, with their history of conquerors, traders and travellers, nearly all of whom have left some impression on culture and consequently on arts and crafts. Many designs or motifs still in use today

AN ORNATELY
CARVED DUSUN BAMBOO
TOBACCO CONTAINER
WITH INTRICATELY
INCISED TRADITIONAL
MOTIFS DECORATING
THE CULM.

have lost their original meaning but remain — albeit transformed — a lingering reminder of a bygone era. Political boundaries are often artificial divisions of people and cultures. In Borneo, they generally mean very little to the indigenous inhabitants, especially those living in the hinterland and on Borneo's coasts. The people of these areas are used to moving freely across borders, with few restrictions. This means that it is sometimes difficult to describe and define a piece of craft, or even a particular design, as being exclusive to a particular ethnic group. For example, certain types of back carriers are made and worn by various ethnic groups living in Sabah, Sarawak, Kalimantan and Brunei. Likewise, the *tikar pandan* — a mat made of *pandan* leaves — is made by coastal communities throughout the Malay Archipelago. The differences are subtle. They include variations in materials, motifs and quality of the handwork, as well as the exact function of the object.

Today, with improved transportation and communications and with the advent of television, cultures from neighbouring countries and even those from further afield play an important part in the development of local material culture. Objects and artefacts were traditionally functional in nature, made for domestic use. Many of these were also personalised creations, lovingly crafted for a specific need and made to last. Tourism and technology have created different needs and niches for hand-crafted objects. The manufacturing process has become more impersonal and perhaps less aesthetically inspired. The craftsperson also produces greater quantities of these objects for a wider market. The underlying problem of such production is the diminishing quality of the crafts, and over time they may begin to look all too familiar, becoming more universal and identical to those produced elsewhere.

At the same time, credit is due to institutions and government agencies such as *Kraftangan Malaysia* (Handicraft Malaysia) of the Malaysian Handicraft Development Corporation, in Kuala Lumpur, and *Koperasi Pembangunan Desa* (Rural Development Corporation) in Sabah, which encourage the development and manufacture of local indigenous crafts and work for a resurgence of good quality artefacts. To all intents and purposes, tourism has been largely responsible for revitalising Malaysia's craft industry.

MALAYSIA'S BOTANICALLY-BASED CRAFTS

Malaysia has been endowed with rich forest, riverine and coastal vegetation, all of which provide abundant supplies of material for crafts made of grass and plant fibres. Many objects are made from a combination of fibres, from jungle creepers, reeds and other vegetable fibres. Many indigenous people in Sabah and Sarawak, like their kindred tribes in the rest of Kalimantan, also use non-vegetable matter, such as shell, bone, metal, stone, glass and clay. In recent years, colourful synthetic fibres, lashings and other plastic material have further decorated their handwork.

Since many crafts made of grass and plant fibres in Malaysia are created from more than one type of material fibre, it is difficult to describe the variety that exists without looking at their plant sources. Attempts to classify these objects can also be made according to their form, function or the methods by which they are made. The most widespread techniques are those of basketry: the weaving, plaiting, twining and coiling of treated leaves, stems and even roots of various plants.

A BAMBOO QUIVER FOR CARRYING BLOW-PIPE DARTS, WITH A WOODEN HANDLE TO HANG ON TO THE HUNTER'S WAIST.

RATTANS AND BAMBOOS

The most commonly used materials for craft making are bamboo (*Gigantochloa spp.*) and several species of rattan (*Calamus spp*). Both bamboo and rattan are strong, light, smooth and straight, allowing length-wise strips to be made from their stems. Of the two, rattan, a solid cane, is the more durable and versatile while still being pliant — qualities desirable for making both baskets and mats.

Rattans belong to the palm family and thrive best in undisturbed rainforests. They are basically climbers, scrambling up to the forest canopy to reach the light, so their stems can be far longer than bamboos are tall. Their value and popularity is due largely to their variety. Rattans range anywhere from 3 mm to 4 cm in diameter, and they can grow up to 200 m in length. Rattans are naturally protected by thorns, spikes and bristles on their stems and leaves. Harvesting rattan is hard work and not particularly pleasant. Collecting is usually done by men who carry the rattans home coiled or cut into sections. The thorny outer skin is stripped to expose the shiny smooth layer, which is the choice material for the outer layer of mats and baskets. The canes most sought after by local people are the *rotan saga* (*Calamus caesius*). These lashings of cane vary in diameter but are seldom bigger than the size of a pencil. Rattans are non-timber forest produce, and depleting forest supplies are now being replaced by rattan plantings by the local people, who take what they need and sell the surplus.

Bamboos, on the other hand, are giant grasses belonging to the *Gramineae* family. In Sabah alone there are no less than 35 species, most of which are used in a variety of ways and in combination with other botanical materials taken from the local environment. Some 10 species are found only in Sabah. Though less hardy, bamboo is perhaps more versatile in the ways it can be used. Its hollow cylindrical stem, or culm, can hold water and gives the bamboo structural strength coupled with a comparatively light weight. There are also a great number of species available, providing a variety of sizes and culm lengths for a multitude of uses, ranging from small domestic implements to housing and construction components. In the Tambunan District of Sabah (where no less than nine species of bamboo are found) there are still whole houses made completely from bamboo, lashed together with the ubiquitous rattan. Another useful property is the bamboo's fast rate of growth. Unlike rattans, bamboos thrive in disturbed open spaces, in forest clearings and along river banks.

For an object made from bamboo to last and resist rapid deterioration from insects, the plant must be harvested and treated in certain ways. Wherever usage of bamboo is widespread, village folk have developed traditional methods of harvesting, evolved from trial and error. The Dusun/Kadazan harvesting formula, an important part of local folk wisdom, has been found to have a sound scientific basis. The Dusun/Kadazan of Tambunan almost never harvest bamboo outside the periods known as *rondom* and *magalang*. *Rondom* literally means 'no moon', a period of time when the bamboo may produce greater amounts of cellulose and silica than of starch, the latter being food for insects. Harvesting during the *magalang* period, when the leaves of the bamboo drop, is also said to produce insect-resistant material. If forced to harvest at other times, village folk leach out bamboo stems or poles in fast-flowing streams for several days to remove their starch.

OTHER PALMS

Other common plants widely used in the production of local crafts belong to the palm family. These are the common coconut tree (*Cocos nucifera*), the *nipa* palm (*Nypa fruticans*), the sago palm (*Metroxylon sagu*), the locally named *polod* (*Arenga undulatifolia*) and *silad* (*Licuala spp.*) and the *pinang* tree (*Areca catechu*). Parts of these trees are used on their own or in a matrix with other materials and fibres. The freshly-cut *lidi*, the leaf vein or spines of *nipa* or coconut, are quickly fashioned into household items called *tampirai* by the Bajau in Sabah, and *leka* by the Malays in Peninsular Malaysia. These were initially made as simple receptacles to hold cooking pots and ceramic objects, but later became fruit baskets and serving containers for cakes. When colour is added to the material these can be used as decorative wall ornaments. Bunches of six to seven *lidi* are coiled and plaited flat while still soft and pliable. These are probably the simplest of baskets, requiring very little preparation and effort.

The leaf spines of these palms are also used as reinforcements or 'threads' to join pieces of leaves together. The attractive dark coloured cellulose trunk material of the *polod* is fashioned into needles, textile weaving heddles, blow-pipe darts and other household implements. The leaves of *silad* or *bertam*, and sago are used with other material to make hats and baskets. The young leaf fronds of *bertam* and similar palms have been cleverly turned into fans by the local people. The bracts or spathes of these palms are also used with other materials to make a variety of baskets. It is not uncommon to use more than one variety of palm leaves to make a particular article.

The Bajau of Kota Belud make colourful conical food covers called *tinduang* or *tudung duang*, made by sewing strips of dyed palm leaves (*serdang, Corypha utan*) in vertical lines, superimposed with appliqued designs around the body and further decorated with small braids of palm leaves at the neck and base. This food cover — the small ones are often mistaken for hats — is made up of two to three layers of leaves sewn together for reinforcement and durability. The middle is usually a coarse layer of coconut leaves, and serves as the foundation. Bamboo and other stiffer materials may be added for strength. Strips of *serdang* leaves form the outer layer, and *nipa* the third inner layer.

PANDANUS

Two varieties of screw pine, the *pandan* and the *mengkuang*, both of which belong to the genus *Pandanus*, provide the basic raw material for many crafts and domestic objects produced by coastal communities in the Malay Archipelago. Some screw pines are common seashore plants which thrive on sandy soils. The shorter and finer leaves of the *pandan* are for making a variety of baskets and fine quality mats. *Mengkuang* produces broader and longer but less pliable leaves, used to make coarser mats and plaited objects.

Mengkuang or *pandanus* plants found growing near traditional coastal settlements are a sign that weavers are at work. Making mats, baskets and other household articles from the leaves of these plants is often women's work in traditional Malay society. For centuries, collecting, preparing and plaiting the leaves has been a spare time activity for these women. The women of Terengganu are particularly renowned for the fine quality of their work and the variety of patterns used, maintaining a tradition of

AN IBAN PADI BASKET OR *RAGA MENARANG*, USED TO CARRY PADI SEED DURING THE SOWING SEASON, ESPECIALLY IN HILL PADI CULTIVATION. THE RIM OF THE BASKET IS MADE FROM EITHER RATTAN OR WOOD AND THE MAIN BODY WOVEN USING RATTAN.

excellent craftsmanship which continues today. The Bajau women in Sabah and their sisters from other kindred groups living on nearby islands also produce excellent *pandan* mats incorporating intricate designs which reflect their historical and cultural links with the neighbouring Philippines.

Like most other processes of preparing vegetable material for craft making, the treatment of *pandan* or *mengkuang* leaves is a labour-intensive activity. The collector has to contend with the stinging thorns on the spine and sides of the *pandan* leaves. The thorns are removed from the freshly cut leaves, which are sun dried or softened over fire and cut into narrow strips using a fine-toothed comb of metal blades fitted on a wooden handle, called *jangka*. The finer the mat or basket to be made, the narrower the strips. The leaves are pulled over a piece of wood, and soaked for two or three days in water that has to be regularly changed to remove the sap and soften the fibres, and sun dried. Boiling them in water also removes the sap and bleaches the fibre. The dried bleached strips are very colour-absorbent and are easily dyed. The availability of inexpensive commercial dyes has given a new colour dimension and artistic expression to the production of crafts from this material.

Whatever the medium, most mats are constructed diagonally, beginning at either a corner or at the centre. With this method, a variety of edges can be formed by deftly folding and tucking the loose ends around the edges of the mat. Terengganu women have several names for these selvages. *Pandan* mats are usually made in two layers, the colour patterned layer backed by a larger undyed piece. Warp and weft are kept at right angles to the edges of the piece when a stiffer material is used for making small pieces, for pattern samples, for place mats for the dining table (a new tourist market) and other ornamental uses.

OTHER PLANTS

The sedge (*Lepironia articulata*), a grass-like plant growing in ponds and water-logged land, is locally known as *bundusan*, and is made into soft mats for sleeping and drying padi by the Murut and Dusun/Kadazan. Scientifically, this plant is not a true grass. The treated and dried fibres are colour-absorbent but only the Murut continue to use colour — nowadays shop-bought aniline dyes — to decorate these mats. The Dusun/Kadazan usually weave or plait them plain.

The *bemban* (*Donax grandis*) is another popular source of material for making mats, hats and baskets. The stem of this herbaceous plant is harvested green, split and treated in much the same way as with bamboo to produce workable strips which can be dried and stored for future use, like rattan. It is softer and less durable, but the dried strips look very similar to rattan. To the untutored eye, baskets made from *bemban* can be mistaken for those made from rattan. Iban women in Sarawak have become adept at weaving mats with undyed *bemban*, using traditional patterns which show up in oblique light, like damasque. *Bemban* are much easier to gather than rattan. They are not as tall as bamboo and usually grow in clumps by river banks. Due to difficulties in getting rattan in their area, the Rungus have resorted to using this material as a rattan substitute for their baskets.

The use of twine from creeping ferns is common, too. The fibres can even be used as the principal ingredient of certain pieces, such as the *linagoh*, produced by the Rungus of Sabah. The Rungus make an

A MURUT TOBACCO PIPE WITH INCISED DESIGNS ON THE BODY. THE RAISED PORTION IS THE BOWL, AND THE METAL PRONG ALLOWS THE PIPE TO BE ATTACHED TO THE LOINCLOTH WHEN NOT IN USE.

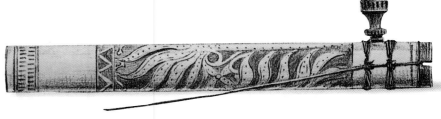

assortment of small baskets and containers by wrapping the stem of a fern which they call *lingkong* (*Lygodium sp.*) in a spiral technique over rattan coils. The form of the pieces is determined by how the coils are stacked. Another useful fern is the *solingkawang* (*Dicranopteris linearis*), which grows in open spaces, hill slopes and degraded soils. The dark-coloured twine found in the stem lends a decorative element when used in combination with light-coloured bleached rattan or bamboo.

BASKETRY

Plant fibres in any environment are the natural material for basket manufacture. Strength, durability and function depend on the materials used. Irrespective of how well-made they are, baskets, mats and other objects deteriorate over time, as their vegetable fibres get subject to wear and tear, mould, rot and other biological damage. They are perishable and so have relatively short lives. But these are essential items. Their basic function as containers has remained unchanged for thousands of years, and their continued production is assured. Archaeological evidence has revealed that baskets have existed since Neolithic times, perhaps developing even before pottery. Perhaps objects made of fibre and using weaving and plaiting processes have persisted for so long because they are generally inexpensive and — almost by definition — within the reach of local people.

For example, among some betel-chewing peoples, small finely-made baskets became practical substitutes for more expensive metal containers which hold betel-chewing ingredients. In fact, in traditional feudal Malay society, basketry was regarded generally as a folk craft and so was associated with the commoners, who were distinguished from the royalty and aristocracy by their material culture.

Unlike textile weaving, basket making is not an entirely female occupation. Although there is some division of labour in the production process, both sexes make baskets, though often of different types. Women weave certain types of baskets, usually smaller and more finely plaited, and principally produced for personal, domestic and other ceremonial purposes. Men, too, produce small baskets, like the Rungus of Kudat district in Sabah with their *solupih*, a little carrier for holding light personal belongings such as tobacco, betel-chewing ingredients and implements. The Tambunan *sosopilon*, a small rattan sling bag, is a good indication of the anomalies that exist in the division of labour. This small shoulder bag is made by men, but usually worn by women. The item, however, has become rare in recent years.

Generally, men make the baskets used for carrying heavy goods. Good examples are the back carriers of various kinds and shapes used to carry hunting spoils, to transport garden or forest produce, and to carry or store grain and other goods. Most big baskets have shoulder straps like a knapsack, with additional straps for the forehead. This is essential when balancing heavy packs while walking in rugged terrain. Where there are no roads or rivers, the tribal folk have to rely on their own physical strength and on the sturdiness of their baskets to move their goods and belongings. Each group or tribe may produce one or more versions of these sturdy carrier baskets, usually also using more than one kind of plant material. All this depends on the availability of the desired material. The stock can be supplemented through trade and barter at the periodic *tamu*, the traditional markets in Sabah. However, the scarcity of

certain kinds of natural fibre, including twine for tying and lashing, has resulted in the use of synthetic substitutes. Raffia and nylon string have gained popularity. Many basket makers in Sabah nowadays prefer to use inexpensive and durable nylon string or fishing line in combination with natural material.

Generally speaking, Sabah and Sarawak share many craft traditions. The same kinds of objects are produced and used by many of the tribal peoples of the East Malaysian states. One of these is the back carrier, called *kalong* (Murut), *selabit* (Iban) and *bakang eet* (Lundayeh or Lun Bawang), woven loosely in a honeycomb pattern using unsplit rattan of the thin wiry variety. This carrier is expandable. The back is made separately either of rattan or even a piece of tree bark, laced to the woven sides. A lid which is an extension of the same woven material is added to the front.

Such a variety of baskets, mats and hats exists in Sabah and Sarawak that it is not possible to do justice to them all. As a rule of thumb, the baskets in Sarawak tend to be reinforced with struts which protrude like little feet, giving them a slightly angular shape at the base. Most of the big baskets in Sabah tend to be circular. The *tekiding*, made from *bemban* and rattan by Bisaya women in Beaufort, is one of the few exceptions. It is reinforced at the four corners, with the splints extending from the narrow base and flaring out to a circular opening. Nearly all the big baskets used for carrying heavier loads have narrow bases and wider mouths. The bases of these baskets are also usually strengthened with coils of woven or unwoven rattan, spathes and other natural woody material. The *buyung* or *saging*, a largely ceremonial basket made by Murut women, is tubular and usually supported on four sides by four rattan rods which meet diagonally at the base. These baskets are usually decorated with motifs similar to those found in Sarawak, representing plants, animals and man in different social relationships.

Murut men sport the small rectangular-shaped flat knapsack called *kapa*, to carry their light personal belongings, the day's food rations, and perhaps the day's catch of fish or meat. These bags — made by women — are usually plain and intended for functional use, but some are created for ceremonial purposes and have elaborate motifs woven in. Another type of bamboo back carrier made by Dusun/Kadazan women is the *sinaging*, which has a round narrow opening and a wider four-cornered base.

As for the Dusun/Kadazan living at the foot of Mount Kinabalu, they make a particularly elegant basket called the *wakid*. This back carrier is cylindrical at the base and has a flared-out top. The body is made of pieces of carefully split bamboo which are tightly fitted at the elongated base. The spokes of the bamboo flare at the mouth of the piece. The ends are secured, lashed individually to two or more rattan hoops using split rattan twine. The body is further reinforced with two or more layers of twine tying the spokes at different heights, which gives a particularly decorative effect. The base is laced with rattan on an overlay of a strip of thin bark. A circular piece of bark lines the bottom of the basket. Usually a spathe is attached to make carrying more comfortable. A pair of shoulder straps made either of woven split rattan or bark cloth and the two ends of a forehead strap flank the spathe to complete the form and function of this basket. The *wakid* is in great demand for its style and grace, as a useful carrier and container, and as a household ornament. *Wakid* are now popular in miniature for the tourist market.

Another handsome carrier made by the Dusun/Kadazan is the *basung*, a circular plan basket made nearly entirely out of spathe, narrow at the base and sewn and tied together by rattan twine. The version with a lid made out of tree bark in combination with the spathe is called a *bongon*. Sarawak, too, has its own versions of finely constructed lidded containers, examples of which are in the Sarawak Museum.

MATS

Some of the finest mats are still made by the Penan people, who have a strong dependency on the natural forests in Sarawak. These mats made of rattan are remarkable for being extremely durable and very finely plaited, but it is the myriad of designs which is truly spectacular, although it is formed from only two colours, a basic black and the colour of the undyed fibre. Other groups in Sabah and Sarawak produce similar mats with similar motifs, but few can compare with the work of the Penan. Their work is so fine that some mats are said to be water-tight.

A 'heavy duty' mat still being made by the indigenous people of both states is the *tikar lampit* (Sabah) or *tikai lampit* (Sarawak). While the plaiting of mats or trays is usually carried out by women as a seasonal activity in between rice-planting seasons, this mat is made by men. Its unique appearance is created by stringing split rods of rattan laid side by side. The ends are bound by braiding rattan twine. Sizes vary from huge floor coverings to rug lengths. These can be rolled but are never folded.

A mat that is no longer used is the seat mat — *tikar burit* — which was worn by the loincloth-clad peoples of Sarawak. It is rectangular in shape, with a pointed end, and is designed to dangle from a man's belt. Made usually of rattan, the mat was sometimes lined with animal skin to provide greater protection from sharp objects wherever the wearer sat. Those made for ceremonial occasions were embellished with beads, cowrie shells, bone and feathers.

Another functional household basketry item is the winnowing tray, which is a shallow pear-shaped or round basket used to remove chaff from the grain. Again, these are made with a combination of two or more plant materials. The surface and rim may be of bamboo, rattan or *bemban*, tied with rattan twine or other fibres. No traditional household is without one, though the uses may have changed. The Rungus now weave small ornamental trays for commercial purposes.

HATS AND OTHER OBJECTS

In East Malaysia more than West, hats are also made from plant fibres, in a profusion similar to that of baskets. The motifs found in mats can be seen also in woven hats. The Murut and Iban have similar conical hats of undyed and dyed split rattan and bamboo in the traditional black and red natural vegetable colours. Other groups sew layers of palm leaves to form wider but flatter hats. These are usually spectacularly decorated with an appliqué of dyed leaves, cloth, beads, shells and other coloured natural and synthetic materials. The *terindak matu* of the Melanau in Sarawak are unusual in that they are made of palm leaves sewn on to umbrella frames of rattan and coloured bamboo. These hats have a mesmerising beauty of their own.

THE MALAY HEXAGONAL WEAVE KNOWN AS *ANYAMAN GILA* ('MAD' WEAVE) IS NOTORIOUSLY DIFFICULT. BASKET WEAVERS NEAR MELAKA HAVE MASTERED THE PRODUCTION OF *ANYAMAN GILA* BOXES FOR THE TOURIST TRADE.

The prize for extremely delicate work must surely go to the few Brunei and Kadazan women of Papar District who make the conical *siung*. A coarsely plaited conical base of bamboo strips is overlaid with tiny thin strands of bamboo, finely woven. These delicate strips are the peelings of a *sumbiling* bamboo (*Schizostachyum lima*) after the green skin has been scraped off. Split rattan rods coloured red are fixed on three sides, each pair flanking the panelled motifs of traditional black and red against an undyed background. The different parts are sewn and secured using rattan twine and fern fibre.

Musical instruments provide a notable use of bamboo. The hollow stems of certain species of the small bamboo make excellent flutes and other aerophones. The most well-known of these is the mouth-organ called the *sompoton* in Sabah. It is made of eight varying lengths of bamboo pipes glued with wax or resin to a dried gourd and tied together with fern fibre or rattan twine. The Lundayeh also make bamboo horn instruments called *bas* which are played in their pipe orchestras. Fish and animal traps made from bamboo and rattan are also very much a feature of rural village life. There are a number of varieties, some simple and some complex, depending on the kind of fish or animal sought.

Incising designs is an interesting technique of decorating bamboo. Even in the past, bamboo containers were rarely left without some imprint of their maker, in the way he tied or fitted the container or in inscriptions of images taken from his life or environment. Designs incised with a sharp pointed blade decorate quivers for blow-pipe darts, tobacco pouches and other bamboo containers. Black colour used to be rubbed into the incisions but red is popular these days. The practice has been revitalised by the demands of the tourist industry.

DYES

Many natural vegetable dyes are being replaced by commercial aniline dyes or paint because of the time and labour involved in making it and because of the scarcity of some of the ingredients needed to produce natural colours. As commercial dyes are generally colour-fast, brighter and offer a variety of hues, it is easy to see why many indigenous people adopt them. The introduction of chemical dyes and other synthetic materials into local craft production has been moderated in recent years by the presence in the craft market of connoisseurs and purists who insist on the authenticity of certain traditional objects, including their colour. The knowledge and skill of extracting colour and dyeing the traditional way are extant and those concerned about keeping cottage industries thriving are also keen to preserve and perpetuate them. The older folk who maintain the dyeing traditions do so out of habit, and perhaps from an innate belief that their ways are still superior. Younger people who place their time at a premium must be encouraged to continue to appreciate natural dyes, at least through art classes at school.

CONCLUSION

Malaysia is diverse and heterogeneous. No less than 32 indigenous groups live in Sabah, with more in Sarawak. Many of these peoples use, make, or were and still are, associated with certain objects which distinguish them from other people. Over the ages, some of these distinctions have mellowed and blended as people borrow and share concepts and production techniques, and use materials from one another. Industrialisation, the development of communications and infrastructure, advances in technology and the advent of modern and mass-produced goods are contributing to a new level of change.

The demand for hand-crafted objects has also altered considerably. A consumer society is steadily replacing the traditional one. However, national pride and practical economic policies are the basis of efforts to preserve and understand Malaysia's living heritage. Traditional craft production is an important part of that heritage, one which is also a valuable economic and cultural resource. Tourism has undoubtedly provided the impetus for the preservation of crafts. But policy makers and implementers must ensure that what is being produced is neither commonplace nor unaesthetic.

Many of the old pieces no longer have any use in people's lives, but not because the functions are no longer needed. In some cases baskets, mats, hats and other objects still retain their utilitarian value and essential forms. The process of manufacturing these items has also basically remained unchanged. It is the materials that have changed. Thus, synthetic twine, discarded nylon bands for packing cases and even cigarette cardboard packs have become raw material. This is not to say that such use of contemporary material has no place in today's society: such works may become tomorrow's traditions. What is crucial is the continuing appreciation of the original works, adequate supplies of the required raw material from the environment, and the opportunity to produce them in the traditional manner.

Craft production in traditional society is inextricably linked to seasonal agricultural or other subsistence activities. This way of life still exists in some rural communities today. More time and more effort may be required to get supplies of raw materials as sources recede deeper into the jungle. The home is still the factory for many of Malaysia's traditional plant fibre-based crafts. It is still basically a spare time activity. Utility is still the premium of production. Form and design have remained remarkably consistent, only styles and materials vary with the inspiration of the creator. When production becomes difficult, these objects are replaced with purchased commercial substitutes. The creation of new markets and a wider appreciative audience who are willing to pay for these products may help to perpetuate these traditions and to encourage creations of high quality.

Many of the old forms are no longer made, their uses having become obsolete. Those that remain are preserved in museums where — appropriately — masterpieces are kept for all to see and appreciate. However, crafts of quality cannot be made just to end up in museums.

Patricia Regis

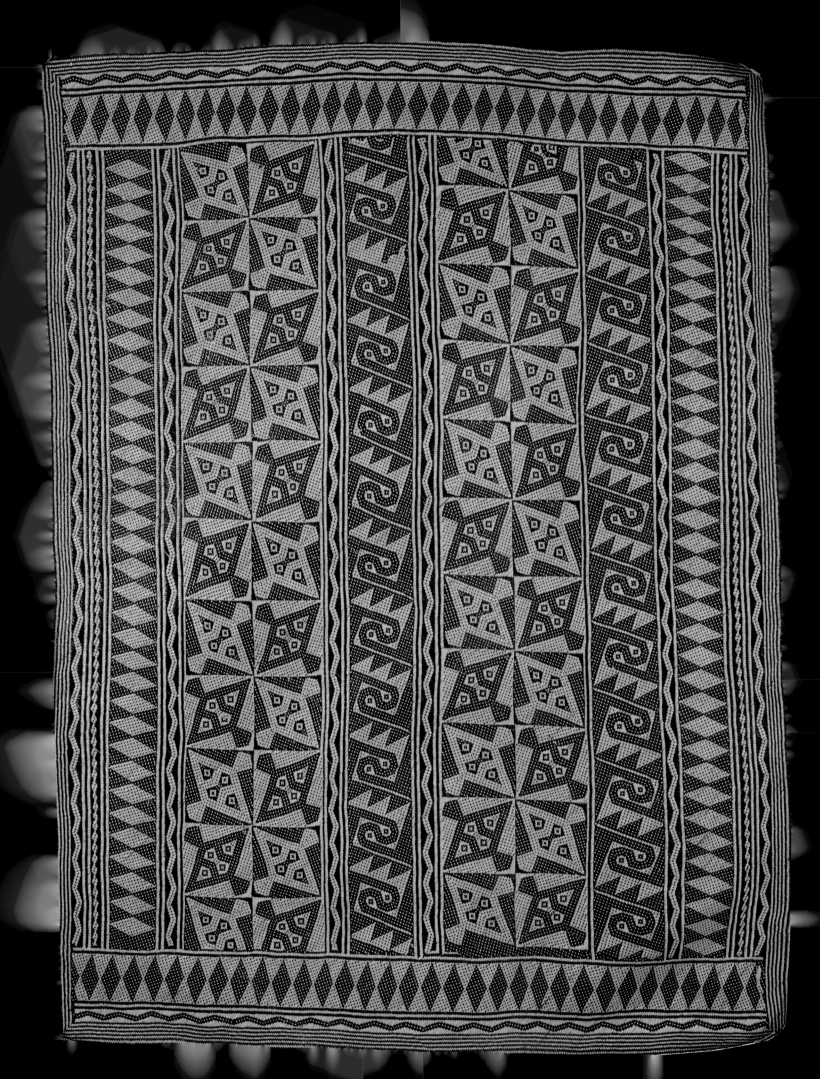

THIS PAGE: PENAN WOMEN PLAITING SLEEPING MATS USING STRIPS OF BLACK DYED AND NATURAL COL-OURED RATTAN, AT THEIR TEMPORARY FOREST SHELTER AT LAYUN, THE UPPER BARAM, SARAWAK. FACING PAGE: A BAMBOO QUIVER TO HOLD BLOW-PIPE DARTS IS AN ESSENTIAL PART OF THE HUNTING EQUIPMENT OF A PENAN HUNTER. HERE IT IS WORN ON THE HIP, WITH ANOTHER BAMBOO CONTAINER FOR OTHER PERSONAL ITEMS STRAPPED ON TO THE OTHER SIDE.

A MURUT WOMAN
WEAVING THIN STRIPS
OF RATTAN, OF NATURAL
COLOURS AND DYED
BLACK, TO PRODUCE
A *BUYUNG*, A SMALL
ORNAMENTAL BACK
CARRIER FOR
CEREMONIAL PURPOSES,
AT KAMPONG SILUNGAI,
DEEP IN THE SOUTH
OF SABAH.

FOOD COVERS ARE
ESSENTIAL PIECES OF
KITCHEN EQUIPMENT IN
TRADITIONAL SOCIETY.
IN THE OLD DAYS THE
MELANAU MADE THEM IN
WOOD CALLED *BON*, BUT
NOWADAYS THESE ARE
MADE FROM RATTAN,
AND SHAPED LIKE
AN UMBRELLA.

A LONGHOUSE IN SABAH
AND SARAWAK IS ALSO
THE VILLAGE FACTORY
FOR PRODUCING BASKETS
AND VARIOUS
HANDCRAFTED ARTICLES.
HERE, TWO BASKET
MAKERS ARE AT WORK
IN THEIR RESPECTIVE
STATES, EACH
PRODUCING HIS OR HER
OWN BRAND OF CRAFTS
WHICH REPRESENT THE
TRIBE. THIS MAN (FACING
PAGE), A BIDAYUH
CRAFTSMAN AT
PEDAWAN, KUCHING,
IS PLAITING A BASKET
WITH A REINFORCED
ANGULAR BASE.
MAKING *LINAGOH*,
SMALL BASKETS USING
THE COILING METHOD,
FOR SALE TO TOURISTS
HELPS SUPPLEMENT THE
FAMILY INCOME FOR THIS
RUNGUS WOMAN
AT KAMPUNG
TINANGOL, KUDAT.

THIS PAGE:
TWO VARIETIES OF
SCREW PINE — THE
PANDAN AND *MENGKUANG*
— PROVIDE THE BASIC
RAW MATERIAL FOR MANY
CRAFTS AND DOMESTIC
OBJECTS PRODUCED BY
COASTAL COMMUNITIES.
FACING PAGE, TOP:
A *PANDAN* MAT FROM
KAMPUNG RUSILA, KUALA
TERENGGANU, INCORPO-
RATING TWO MOTIFS
CALLED *CHE KEDAH* AND
PUCUK REBUNG (BAMBOO
SHOOT), AND (BOTTOM)
ANOTHER *PANDAN* MAT,
ALSO FROM KAMPUNG
RUSILA, WITH A TARTAN
BACKGROUND AND
INCORPORATING SMALL
MOTIFS IN A DESIGN
CALLED *SAMBAS*, WHICH
PROBABLY HAS ITS
ORIGINS IN A TOWN AND
DISTRICT OF THE SAME
NAME IN WEST BORNEO.
FOLLOWING PAGES:
A PRAYER MAT FROM
KAMPUNG RUSILA, MADE
OF *PANDAN*, WITH THREE
MOTIFS INTRICATELY
WOVEN IN CALLED
KELAKAI, *CHE KEDAH* AND
PUCUK REBUNG.

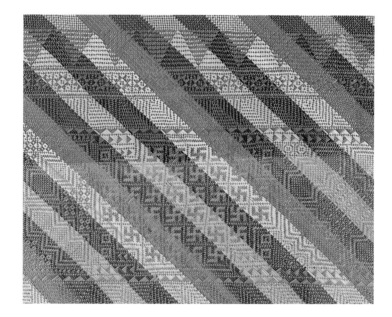

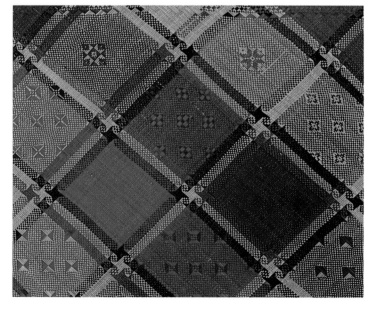

WOOD

It all began with a tree. According to Kayan mythology and the beliefs of other Bornean groups of people, the Tree of Life was the origin of man. Even today traditional workers of wood, whether house- or boat-builders, carvers, or makers of other objects, respect and handle wood with care.

The carver's art is found in all parts of Malaysia, the products of its diverse peoples. The aesthetics vary according to purpose, from the exquisite panels of Malay royal residences, carved with floral motifs and Koranic verses, to the less refined small anthropomorphic statues found in some of the rice fields of Malaysian Borneo. A staggering range of objects are carved from wood, including musical instruments, celebratory objects like the Melanau burial poles of Sarawak, and the carved handles and sword sheaths, *sarong pedang*, of the Bajau in Sabah. The carvings of two of the orang asli groups of the Peninsula are also well known. The Jah Hut of Pahang carve elaborate figures representing forest and household spirits, while the Mah Meri of Carey Island in Selangor are known for their ritual masks.

Today, over sixty percent of Malaysia is still covered in untouched forest. In earlier times, of course, the forest cover was far more extensive. Wood, a versatile and in many cases durable material, comes in enormous variety, with over 3,000 different timber species found in Malaysia. This means that craftsmen — past and present — have many choices for the production of a wide range of wood-based objects. It is not possible to say at which time in history the highly decorative forms of carving that we see today began. They are still being made in many parts of Malaysia. Unadorned objects for utilitarian use — eating utensils, agricultural implements and boats — probably preceded carved ones. Early decorations may have begun as symbols based on nature or mythical creatures with perceived special powers to ward off evil elements in the environment. In Sarawak, the seemingly abstract motifs adorning shields, carved doors, columns and log stairs in some longhouses, and even tattoo forms are based on designs to ward off dangerous spirits. The carvings we see today represent a mixed heritage of older motifs and new ideas and forms brought about by changing external influences.

It would be impossible to do justice to all the wood carving traditions and aesthetics in Malaysia. What follows, therefore, focuses on the Malay tradition. In Peninsular Malaysia, religious belief has had an important influence on art and craft, beginning with animism and culminating, for the Malays, with the advent of Islam in the 14th and 15th centuries. Malay architecture has spiritual, ethical and cultural values and reflects man's appreciation for his environment. This is best exemplified by the embellishments still found today in many homes, particularly carvings.

DESIGN PRINCIPLES

The basic design principle that governs Malay carvings is called *awan larat*. Although the term *awan larat* can be translated literally as 'stretching clouds', it is a metaphor for the flow of the dancer's hands, of life, and of nature. It is also a reflection of Islamic philosophy. It is more than a simple set of rules governing the patterns and designs of Malay artefacts. It is a generic term which subsumes a number of other special forms. The rules and the underlying ethical and aesthetic values of *awan larat* are passed on by example and practice from one generation to the next.

PRECEDING PAGES: WITH LEAVES, SEED PODS AND FLOWERS THAT SEEM TO EBB AND FLOW WITH LIFE AND VITALITY, THIS CARVING IS A TRIBUTE TO THE MASTER CRAFTS-MAN'S SKILL. A BEAUTIFUL EXAMPLE OF *AWAN LARAT*, NOTICE HOW THE FLORAL ELEMENTS ARE SYMMETRICALLY BALANCED AROUND A CENTRAL AXIS, AS ARE THE VOIDS BETWEEN THE CARVED PORTIONS. FACING PAGE: THE HANDS OF A MASTER AT WORK. HERE, HAJI WAN SU WORKS ON A TRADITIONAL FLORAL MOTIF. WORKING IN CHENGAL WITH TOOLS HE MAKES HIMSELF, NOTICE HOW HE ACHIEVES CONTROL BY HOLDING HIS KNIFE BETWEEN HIS THUMB AND FIRST FINGER.

There are four rules governing *awan larat*, according to Wan Mustafa Wan Su, son of a famous wood carver: 1) The spaces have to be the same, that is, the elements must be evenly distributed over the composition; 2) the voids, or spaces between the elements of the composition, must be approximately the same size as the carved elements. This is consistent with the rules for Islamic art in which the 'real' or apparent appearance of an image is balanced with its hidden character or 'void', both elements requiring emphasis. 3) The elements must be plants, whether real or imaginary. Traditional Malay wood carvings never include images of humans or animals. This, again, is consistent with the generally accepted Islamic view about the form of representational images. Plant motifs are central to the sacred art of Islam. 4) When there is a central motif, or *ibu*, such as a flower, leaf, branch or vase, the design must be repeated around it. The carvings which result from the application of these rules are generally plants that are spirally, creepy or extended, with leaves, flowers and buds.

Wan Mustafa has described *awan larat* as falling into three categories: 1) designs which give advice about Godliness through carving, or to teach the coming generation about religion. This kind of carving often has a specific meaning, whether literally spelt out in Koranic verse, or encoded in the symbols of a complex winding of tendrils and shoots of plants; 2) designs which please the eye through the creation of *awan larat* that are beautiful but without meaning. This kind of carving, he said, is easier to create than the first; 3) designs which show reverence to plants as creatures of God. In Malay society there is still a desire to show appreciation to 'useful' plants. Plants are the basis of design for all *awan larat*. In addition to edible plants, useful flora include a wide range of medicinal plants. Sometimes a patron favours a particular type of plant. The last Raja of Patani is said to have been fond of breadfruit, or *sukun* (*Artocarpus incisus*), and that decorating his palace were many carvings depicting the leaves of the *sukun* tree.

There is an example of a carving imbued with meaning which used to be easily accessible to the public. It was in a small traditional Malay house on stilts, called 'Rumah Seri Tanjung', built as a display on a promontory, or *tanjung*, in Lake Titiwangsa, Kuala Lumpur. The house has since been dismantled. Above the inside door, in the space called the *jejala*, was a three-panelled fenestrated carving, carved both front and back so that it could be viewed from either side, which made it unusual. The carving was done by Wan Mustafa and his father, Wan Su. The central motif, or *ibu*, was a flower called *bunga tanjung*. The *bunga tanjung* was made in the shape of a large circle to represent a lake. The choice of this flower had significance in three ways. First, the place where the house was sited was a *tanjung*. Next, the *bunga tanjung* is the name of a famous traditional song. And lastly, *bunga tanjung* represents *wangsa*, which means the descendants of good people, or *bangsawan*. This is to remind people to conduct themselves properly. Every leaf was curved so that it did not touch, or push into any other leaf. This illustrates the Malay cultural precept of not disturbing or abusing anyone else. Each 'younger' tendril arose underneath an 'older' one, illustrating the carver's advice for young people to honour those who are more senior to them in age or position. The flowers which arose above the central *bunga tanjung* were meant to convey the idea that Malay culture should be upheld and its sanctity preserved. It is clear that Islam permeated the carvers' design and interpretation, as it has for many generations.

The earliest Malay settlements were along coastal areas in the north — in Patani, Kelantan, Terengganu and Kedah. The interior was jungle. Life was in harmony with nature, and an ecological balance was maintained. The forest was the source of food, medicine and building materials. Master craftsmen, boat- and house-builders knew and respected the trees that supplied their basic needs. The sea was an important part of life, too, as was the building of boats to harvest the sea's bounty and to explore further. Boats capable of long journeys sailed from the Terengganu coast and could have gone as far as Egypt in the 1st century AD. Terengganu appeared on a map of the Malay Peninsula attributed to Ptolemy in the 2nd century. Two cities are named, Perimoula at the mouth of the Terengganu River and Kole, which was probably Kemaman. Both are still important East Coast ports for fishing fleets.

Virtually none of the great Malay sailing vessels exist today, apart from two that plied the trade route from Terengganu to Siam, with stops at Pulau Perhentian. These are now on exhibit onshore at Losong, Kuala Terengganu. When they attacked Melaka and later Kota Lama in Johor, the Portuguese stated that they encountered fleets of as many as 2,000 Malay sailing craft, and they described local ships as large as 1,000 tons, more than twice as large as any Portuguese craft of the time.

Even before the rise of Melaka, the Malay states had a long history of contact with the great civilisations of China, whose boats sailed south with the north-east monsoon winds. There was also early influence from Indochina, Champa and the Khmer kingdoms. These contacts influenced Malay culture and architecture a great deal, particularly on the East Coast and Kedah. Only in Terengganu, Kelantan and Kedah is found the shadow play or *wayang kulit*. Intricate metal- and silversmithing, *pandan* mat weaving, songket weaving, Ma'Yong dance drama, traditional kite flying and the carving of giant spinning tops are still specialties of the East Coast. It is also on the East Coast that one finds the intricate filigree wood carvings on houses and old palaces, an art Malays call *sobek*.

CHOOSING THE RIGHT WOOD

How did craftsmen obtain their wood, and what kinds did they choose? Even as recently as a hundred years ago, the craftsmen went directly to the forest for their supply. The father of Latif Long, a well-known carver now working in Kelantan, En. Long Yussof of Besut Terengganu, and the generation of master craftsmen who preceded him, were among them. A group of men consisting of craftsmen (and in some cases the prospective owner of the house or boat), helpers and a *pawang* or *bomoh* would go into the forest with provisions and equipment for up to three months, to seek the trees that would yield the wood they needed. The *pawang* was skilled in the incantations needed to ward off evil or dangerous spirits. All the men had faith in God and had since young memorised special Islamic prayers that would ensure peaceful sleep at night. These prayers, called *ilmu pagar* (literally 'fence knowledge'), protected them from the wild game, elephants, bears and tigers that lived in the jungle.

Timing was important. The search had to be conducted in dry months, and completed late enough for rivers to have risen sufficiently to float wood downstream, but not so late that the monsoon season had started. These were men who truly understood and lived in harmony with nature. Suitable trees were

THIS DRAGON-LIKE DOG WITH A LONG SNOUT, CURLING FANGS AND HORNS IS A COMMON SUBJECT OF CARVINGS BY BOTH THE KAYAN AND KENYAH OF SARAWAK. KNOWN AS AN ASO, IT PLAYS AN IMPORTANT PART IN RELIGION. CARVED SINGLY, OR AS SUPPORTING ELEMENTS FOR PLATES AND TABLES, THE ASO MOTIF IS ALSO COMMONLY FOUND IN TATOOS AND PAINTINGS.

eventually identified. If the tree was Chengal (*Balanocapus heimii*), a hard dense wood favoured by house builders, boat builders, and carvers, it would be tested first to ensure its suitability, by making an incision around the trunk. If sap did not flow freely it was an old tree that would yield good quality wood. Before the selected tree could be cut down the spirits of the forest, *jenggi kayu*, had to be propitiated first.

Felling the tree took another kind of expertise. The tree itself, and the wood that it yielded, was honoured in its own right. It was said to have *semangat*, or vital force, a concept predating Islam but accepted even now by traditional craftsmen. Old trees were of sufficient girth that a platform had to be erected for the cutter to work, since the girth of the base would be too large. In early times a flexible axe was the main cutting tool, one still in use in some orang asli communities. The direction of fall also had to be considered. The aim was to ensure minimal damage to surrounding trees when the cut tree fell. It could take up to two or three days to fell one tree. Two-man hand saws came later, and even then could require a day or more of cutting time. Once the tree was felled there remained the task of cutting the tree into suitable sizes and of taking it out of the jungle. If the tree was some distance from a river, the wood had to be moved overland until a river was reached. Buffalo were used for this purpose, except in special cases, as when a royal palace was being built, in which case the sultan would provide his elephants for the work. The actual building was generally done by Malay craftsmen, sometimes with the help of skilled Chinese, who have had a long history of settlement on the East Coast.

Only in a few rare cases today have master builders gone into the jungle to identify and fell trees to build a house. Possibly the most recent and perhaps last example occurred in the construction of a house built by hand from Chengal in the Sepang District of Selangor in the last eight years. The builders, Kelantanese, led by master carpenter Ibrahim Adam, selected three trees — two from the Gua Musang area of Kelantan and one from Hulu Besut in Terengganu. The trees were felled in the jungle and brought out by tractor and lorry to a sawmill in Pasir Puteh, Kelantan, to be cut into suitable sizes.

The house itself was largely constructed without the use of nails, using *tebuk pasak* or mortise and tenon construction. The average age of the workers who built the house was sixty. Younger men seem uninterested, or lack the patience to serve the apprenticeship required to learn the necessary skills of these master builders. The house took six-and-a-half years to complete. Without patrons willing to wait for the building of such houses, and without a new generation of such skilled workers, it is unlikely that many more such houses will be built. Respect for the wood was always evident. In one case, three wall studs of Resak wood (*Otylelobium spp.*) were put into place in an otherwise fully Chengal house. When Ibrahim the master carpenter was asked why, his reply was that *"Chengal merupakan Raja, mesti ada rakyat"*. ("Chengal represents the royalty, there must be ordinary people".)

DIFFERENT TYPES OF WOOD

Chengal is only one of many other woods used in house- or boat-building. For a royal palace, Chengal might provide for almost all needs — supporting pillars, floors, walls, wall studs, rafters — perhaps everything except the roof. For a more usual dwelling, a number of different kinds of woods would be

used for specific purposes in construction. Among these woods is Balau (*Shoria materialis*), favoured for supporting pillars (*tiang*), for connecting members that supported the floor and fitted into the *tiang*, called *rasuk*, for roof joists (*alang*), rafters (*kasau jantan*), roof supports or *tunjuk langit*, and ridge poles or *tulang bumbung*. Resak is used for much the same purpose, being only slightly softer than the Chengal. Perah (*Elateriospernum tapos*) and Sepetir (*Sindora spp.*) are used for floors and walls.

Many other kinds of wood have been used in house building, most for similar purposes to those above. Which wood is used depends on availability, and what the prospective owner can afford. Clearly local craftsmen know the forest well. Many of these types of woods are still being used to build rural wooden houses, although such houses are being built less and less as time passes.

Some other kinds of wood used include Betis (*Palaquium sp.*), Damar Laut (*Canarium hirsutum*), Keruing (*Vafica scortechinii*), Kulim (*Scorodocarpus borneesis*), Kapur (*Depohalanops aromatica*), Meranti (*Shoria Sp.*) and many more. Some hardwoods like Merbau (*Intsia sp.*), and Rengas (*Gluta Spp.*), while theoretically suitable for supporting pillars, are rarely used. According to Malay belief Merbau is haunted and therefore unsuitable for use in any part of the house, while Rengas is believed to contain poisonous sap.

Chengal is never treated, except with *damar minyak*, a termite resistant varnish. Once the house is finished, or during its construction, other craftsmen would begin their work. These are the master carvers, bearers of skills handed down to selected members of succeeding generations. Today's skilled carvers are heirs to these men, who built the grand palaces and extraordinary houses of past times. At present only a handful of these structures survive. Some have succumbed to the ravages of tropical weather, while others were destroyed in fires, in warfare, or more recently simply neglected because they are no longer valued. Some have even been torn down and used as firewood.

Because of its description in the *Malay Annals*, the best known Malay palace or istana was that built by Melaka's Sultan Mansor Shah around 1465. Although the *Malay Annals* were written several decades after the event, the author could vividly remember its construction and subsequent rebuilding after it was destroyed in a disastrous fire. It was described as a magnificent structure containing many carvings, with a seven-gabled roof, gilded spires and even Chinese mirrors. The fact that it could be rebuilt within a year of the fire is an indication of the level of skilled craftsmanship of that period. The palace was destroyed again by the Portuguese in 1511 and a partial replica has been rebuilt in Melaka. It includes roof tiles of Belian (*Eusideroyxlon zwageri*), an ironwood imported from its native habitat in Sarawak. Belian is Malaysia's hardest wood, reaching densities of between 800-1,100 kilogrammes per cubic metre.

One of the most recent wooden palaces to be built was that at Seri Menanti in the state of Negri Sembilan. Built during the first part of this century, it contains carvings on 26 of its pillars and a carved verandah border extending 38m. The verandah carving includes some mythical creatures, probably designed by a Chinese craftsman from Melaka, as typically Malay carvings are based on plants. Only the Malays embellish their houses with carvings of the quality found in their palaces and homes. Such carvings are not found in the homes of any other ethnic group in Malaysia. The finest wood carvers are still found on the East Coast, in Terengganu and Kelantan.

KLIRENG, OR WOODEN BURIAL POLES FOR THE BURIAL OF ARISTOCRATS, WERE CARVED BY THE PENAN BAH WHO, UNLIKE THE NOMADIC PENAN, ARE A SETTLED COMMUNITY ON THE UPPER BAH RIVER IN SARAWAK. AS MANY AS FIVE HUNDRED MEN WOULD BE INVOLVED IN THE CARVING OF SUCH POSTS, WHICH REACH HEIGHTS OF 6-7 METRES.

MODERN-DAY WOOD CARVERS

One such person is Nik Rashidin Haji Husein. He is in his mid-thirties and lives and works in Kota Bharu, Kelantan. His first love is making the hilt, *hulu*, and sheath, *sarong*, of the kris, the traditional Malay dagger whose qualities and power are believed to be mystical. As a measure of the quality of his work, kris that he has made have been selected three times by the Government of Malaysia as official gifts. Recipients have included Ronald Reagan, former President of the United States, President Suharto of Indonesia, and the Brunei royal family. He makes no kris to order, and regards kris making as an expression of his cultural heritage and identity. His aim is to produce kris in as close an approximation as possible to the form and way that they have been made traditionally, using the techniques and even finishes of natural gums obtained from the forest. He has also made other kinds of carvings, including raised (*timbul*) and fenestrated (*tebuk*) carvings of Koranic verses, as well as the massive main gate to the Balai Besar, the Royal Meeting Hall, in Kota Bharu.

Nik Rashidin's ancestors come from Patani and Kelantan and include many craftswomen. His maternal grandmother was a goldsmith working in Kampong Langgar. Skilled goldsmiths often made the fenestrated carvings at the upper portion of palace walls, or the *sobek* or *rupur* at the edge of the roof. Such carvings can be seen today at Rumah Tele, a Terengganu palace on display at the site of the Terengganu State Museum at Losong, Kuala Terengganu. Other relatives were songket weavers. Nik Rashidin is also related to Tengku Ibrahim Tengku Wok, whose mother, Nik Boh, was Nik Rashidin's paternal grandmother's sister. Tengku Ibrahim, who lives near the town of Jerteh, in Terengganu, is a carver whose work is done in exquisite detail.

Born in his grandfather's house in Wakaf Siku, Kota Bharu, Nik's mother was a *bangsawan*, a noblewoman. She frequently took young Nik with her from place to place. At a very young age, he remembers being fascinated by a carved *kukur kelapa*, a coconut scraper carved in the shape of a horse. Later, he would spend hours looking at kris on display in shop windows along Jalan Merbau. Convinced that he could reproduce them himself, he began trying his hand at the craft. In school, he excelled in crafts and his L.C.E. (Lower Certificate of Education) carving project won first prize at the national level. He wanted to continue carving instead of pursuing his schooling.

Initially with his own funds, later reluctantly supplemented by his father, Nik went to a famous school for carvers at Jepara on Central Java's north coast. Unfortunately, the school was academically oriented and directed to furniture making, devoting only one hour a week to practical work. Nik increasingly stayed away from school and instead visited old mosques to study their carvings. He sought out master craftsmen to try and learn from them, even going as far afield as Bali. After a year in Indonesia he returned to Kota Bharu and received his only formal practical training in carving as a worker for the then young Latif Long. He worked in Latif's workshop for about three years. It was also during this time, around 1973, that he met Wan Su Othman, the now well-known master carver from Alor Lintang, Besut, Terengganu. They met at the workshop of Cikgu Mohamad Abu Bakar, in Kota Bharu. Wan Su was visiting to share his carving skills and knowledge of the intricate *awan larat* designs.

AN UNUSUAL CAKE MOULD OR *ACUAN*, FOR MAKING TRADITIONAL SWEETS CALLED *PUTU KACANG*, USUALLY MADE FROM FLOUR GROUND FROM MUNG BEANS. IN THIS MOULD THE PATTERN CONSISTS OF LEAVES INTER-CONNECTED AT THE BOTTOM, WHILE MORE COMMONLY EACH FORM IN THE MOULD WOULD BE INDEPENDENT OF THE OTHER.

Here then, in Kota Bharu, a community of traditional wood carvers came together. One, Latif, the direct descendent of a master carpenter and craftsman, and the other two the young Nik Rashidin and the much older Wan Su, each descended from craft-making lineages. Between them, these carvers have produced masterpieces of carving, continuing the tradition for which the East Coast is especially known.

Nik Rashidin was forced to stop his work with Latif Long when he fell ill and was unable to work for several years. During this time, he dreamed of getting the ideal woods for kris handles and sheathes. In the meantime he dressed *golok*, small dagger-like knifes that do not require special wood. He particularly desired Kemuning, a yellow wood from the roots of the *Murraya paniculata*, with a beautiful grain. This grain is unusual, a quirk of the Murraya's development, as most tropical trees show no growth rings. He also required Sena (*Pterocarpus indicus*) and Chengal for other types of carvings. He got a small amount of Kemuning and Sena from Tengku Ibrahim, and began to work under his father's house. In 1983 he heard that some wood of the kind he needed for kris making was for sale in Batu Rakit, Terengganu. He bought 55 pieces, some as large as a man's thigh and cut to lengths of more than a metre. This hoard and additions to it will keep him in work for the rest of his life. Nik Rashidin stores the wood in a dry place and will not use a piece until it has dried for seven or eight years. It is only in this way that he can ensure that his kris will match the quality of the tradition he seeks to maintain.

One very rare type of wood that he uses he calls 'Kenaung'. If freshly cut, the wood is white, but when the tree has died and fallen, it undergoes a transformation that, after some years, causes the heartwood to turn as black as coal. Nik treasures his small supply. He now works at home, together with his younger brother Nik Rashidi, a fine carver in his own right but entirely trained by his elder brother, and constantly encouraged by his wife Rosmawati Othman. The brothers treat their wood with reverence. They believe that it has the vital force called *semangat*. The kris blades Nik uses have been collected throughout the Malay Archipelago. Made by master ironsmiths, they are perfect matches for the *hulu* and *sarong* he makes so beautifully. His travels and studies have made him an acknowledged expert on kris, and he is now visited often by scholars from such diverse places as China and Italy.

At age 96, another master craftsman, Haji Wan Su Othman, spent three months completing a marvellous bird cage made from Kayu Nangka, the wood of the Jackfruit (*Artocarpus heterophyllus*). He and his wife have made the pilgrimage to Mecca twice, most recently when he was 93. This gentle man carved the doors of the National Museum in KL in 1963. He has lived and worked for many years in the small kampung of Alor Lintang on the road between Jerteh and Kampung Raja in the Besut District of Terengganu. Although of Patani descent, he was born and spent his early childhood in Pengkalan Kubor, in the Tumpat District of Northern Kelantan. He has been a boat builder and maker of *wau*, Malay kites and *patung wayang kulit*, the Ramayana shadow play puppets made of water buffalo hide. This illustrates another characteristic of many master craftsmen — their versatility. His workshop until recently was called 'Balai Seni Ukir WanSu', (the Woodcarving Centre of WanSu). He has passed the workshop onto one of his sons, Wan Mustafa, a master carver who learned from his father the art he now practises. The workshop is now called 'Balai Seni Wan Mustafa WanSu', (the Arts Centre of Wan Mustafa WanSu).

FACING PAGE, TOP: IN A SIMPLE WORKSHOP LOCATED UNDER HIS HOUSE NEAR THE TOWN OF JERTEH IN TERENGGANU, TENGKU IBRAHIM TENGKU WOK CARVES OBJECTS OF GREAT INTRICACY AND DETAIL. HANDLES FOR THE MALAY KRIS, BOXES AND WALKING STICKS ALL TAKE MONTHS OF PAINSTAKING WORK TO COMPLETE. BOTTOM: RELATED TO TENGKU IBRAHIM TENGKU WOK, NIK RASHIDIN HAJI HUSEIN, A RELATIVELY YOUNG CARVER, HAS ACHIEVED A VERY HIGH DEGREE OF SKILL. HIS CARVINGS RANGE FROM THE MASSIVE GATES TO THE BALAI BESAR IN KOTA BHARU, TO EXQUISITELY CARVED TRADITIONAL KRIS HANDLES AND FINELY MADE HILTS

None of Wan Mustafa's own children have followed in his footsteps and taken up carving. This does not, however, herald the end of a line of carvers, for two reasons: First, both Haji Wan Su and Wan Mustafa have trained a large number of apprentices, some of whom have gone on to open their own workshops; and secondly, they are ever willing to give help and guidance to their apprentices and to those with interest in carving. They do not see the success of their students as a threat. Rather, they view it as a perpetuation of their traditional craft and skills.

One former apprentice, who was also apprenticed to Tengku Ibrahim, is one of three master carvers commissioned by the new Terengganu State Museum at Losong. Norhaizah Nordin helped complete the carving of doors, wall panelling and stairways. Working with him were Wan Mustafa and Latif Long, and so again the intertwining of the lives of the master carvers continues. Wan Mustafa did the carvings of one of the main entrance doors, as his father had done before for another museum.

A craft lineage can be carried on if, as sometimes happens, a grandchild continues with the tradition. In Malay society there is a special love and tolerance of grandchildren. Sometimes when a craftsman is meticulous in his work and the care of his tools, he will reprimand a son who intrudes into his domain, but will allow a grandchild to play in his presence and even handle his tools.

AN ENDURING TRADITION

The carvings of Haji Wan Su and his son Wan Mustafa are found today in royal palaces, mosques, and in the private collections of lovers of traditional crafts in Malaysia and overseas. It was only in the last fifteen years, however, that any part of Haji Wan Su's own house was embellished with carvings. The traditional patrons of carvers in the past were royal families or families of wealth and position, most often connected to the court. Carvers rarely received payment as such, but were supported with food and shelter while on the job. Occasionally, the carver would be given wood. This would be particularly so if the work involved a renovation, where perhaps an existing wall was to be replaced with a carving. The original wall might be given to the carver. It would never occur to the carver to embellish his own house with carvings, no matter how much he himself might value such works. And value carvings they did, so as times and patrons change it now seems no longer inappropriate to embellish one's own house. Haji Wan Su's house has many carvings. The front doors are carved with the Arabic script for *Allahu Akhbar*, God is Great. Above the doors leading into the inside rooms, the wall partitions do not reach the ceiling. As is customary in rural Malay houses, open carved panels, *tebuk*, are placed above the doors, allowing for air circulation. Haji Wan Su now has carvings above the doors and an elaborately carved central pillar in the centre of his large front room.

Not far from the workshops of Haji Wan Su and Wan Mustafa, Tengku Ibrahim Tengku Wok works beneath his house close to the Terengganu town of Jerteh. This quiet and gentle man, the descendent of Malay princes, carves kris hilts, walking sticks or *tongkat*, and exquisite boxes fit for the crown jewels. It was Tengku Ibrahim who originally supplied the precious wood that his young relative, Nik Rashidin, needed to get started. Nik Rashidin, Haji Wan Su, Wan Mustafa and Tengku Ibrahim are

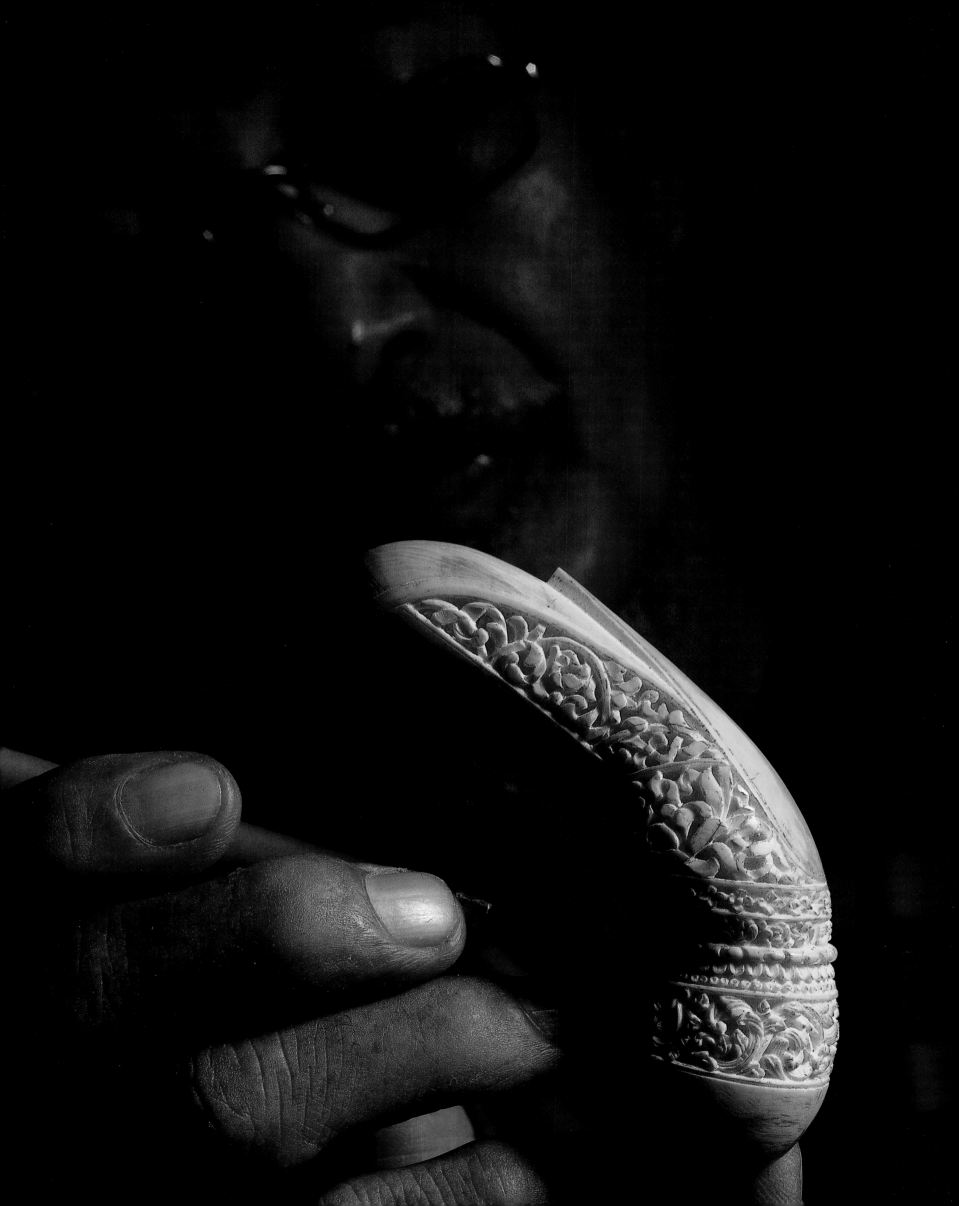

traditionalists. They work the way their predecessors used to, with tools they make themselves and carving traditional forms according to the rules passed down from one generation to the next. Latif Long, on the other hand, although still producing many traditionally shaped carvings, is a semi-traditionalist from the point of view of production techniques and business practice. His business can now be fairly described as commercial. He works in a very large workshop employing large numbers of workers. He practises a form of 'assembly line' approach were work is subdivided so that different workers do different jobs. Some cut wood, others draw and fix plans to wood, and yet others carry out carving, sanding and finishing. Latif, assisted by his brother Abdul Rahman, supervises, and if necessary, touches up the final product. Customers can now choose from pre-prepared patterns which are traditional, modern, or both. Latif Long himself has stated that wood carvings need not necessarily be tied to ancient designs, and he has incorporated new plant forms or combinations of forms into his carvings. The quality remains, however — a lesson well learnt from his master craftsman father.

Other changes are taking place in the use of wood to produce objects for enjoyment, utilitarian and tourist uses. Kraftangan, a Malaysian quasi-governmental agency, is pioneering the production of wood products that are traditional in form but made for a mass market, both locally and overseas. This agency is also exploring entirely new forms. The production of these objects is being encouraged on a commercial scale, in part to make the public more aware of crafts. Kraftangan also encourages traditional craftsmen, both by inviting them to teach their craft to young people and through a special programme called 'Adihguru', which recognises master craftsmen and supports them financially for specified periods. Kraftangan also manages a craft museum in Kuala Lumpur known as 'Infokraf'. On display in this museum are modern forms in traditional materials, such as wood. The commercial sector, often with the support of the Malaysian Timber Industry Board of the Ministry of Primary Industries, has also been active in producing wood products for both local and overseas use. Modern furniture is being made by a number of firms, using Malaysian hardwoods such as Sepetir, Balau, Ramai, Kambong Samangkok and Nyatoh. A wood that is now being used for furniture and other purposes is Rubberwood, which is harvested when old plantations are replanted or replaced with other agricultural products.

As the 21st century approaches, wood is still being used as a primary raw material for the production of a wide variety of objects, and is likely to continue to be used. Existing side-by-side are modern, semi-traditional and traditional uses of wood. Each has its place. Traditional craftsmen and their art, however, must remain and be encouraged, an increasingly difficult task given the pressures of progress. Fortunately, there are still the lovers of things traditional, and a small but growing number of patrons willing to support the master craftsman's art. What is needed now is a balance between these three approaches. A total shift to either a semi-traditional or modern approach to the use of wood runs the risk of destroying a cultural heritage that has its roots in history and gives identity to its people.

Rudin Salinger

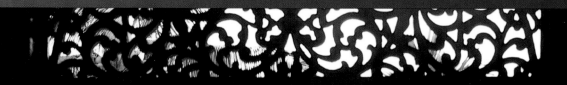

THIS PAGE: A PENAN
FROM THE UPPER BARAM
RIVER IN SARAWAK
CUTS WOOD WITH A
FLEXIBLE HANDLED ADZE.
WHEN THE ADZE IS
RAISED BEFORE STRIKING
A BLOW, THE FLEXIBLE
HANDLE CARRIES IT
BACKWARDS, SO THAT
AS IT IS BROUGHT
DOWN ITS MOMENTUM
IS GREATER, LEAVING
A DEEP CUT IN
THE WOOD.

FACING PAGE: CARVED
CIRCA 1870 FROM THE
VERY HARD WOOD
KNOWN AS BELIAN, THIS
DETAIL FROM A BURIAL
POLE SHOWS TWO
MONSTERS AND
TRADITIONAL MOTIFS,
COMMISSIONED BY AYUN
DIAN OF ULU BELAGA,
SARAWAK. IT SUPPORTS A
BURIAL HUT AT ITS TOP
AND WAS DESIGNED TO
HOLD HIS DAUGHTER'S
REMAINS. IT NOW STANDS
IN THE GROUNDS OF THE
SARAWAK MUSEUM.

THIS PAGE: THESE ENTWINED FIGURINES ARE MADE OF SOFT WOOD BY THE MELANAU CARVERS OF SARAWAK. USED AS SICKNESS SPIRITS OR *BLUM*, THEY ARE CARVED IN THE LIKENESS OF TWO SICK PERSONS. ON COMPLETION, THE IMAGE WOULD BE PLACED IN A DECORATED MODEL BOAT AND SENT DOWNSTREAM WITH ITS OWNER'S ILLNESS, HOPEFULLY NEVER TO RETURN. FACING PAGE: CARVED BY AN ORANG ASLI CRAFTSMAN OF THE JAH HUT GROUP IN CENTRAL PAHANG, THIS DELIGHTFUL PAIR ARE KNOWN AS *BES KEMOIT KEMBAR. BES KEMOIT* IS A SPECIAL DEITY WHILE *KEMBAR* IS A MALAY WORD MEANING TWIN. THE CARVING IS FROM RED MERANTI.

EACH OF THE THREE
HULU KRIS, OR KRIS
HANDLES, ILLUSTRATED
HERE HAS SPECIAL
CHARACTERISTICS AND
DIFFERENT ORIGINS.
ALTHOUGH WOOD IS
OFTEN USED IN THE
CARVING OF THESE
OBJECTS, *GADING* (IVORY)
IS ALSO USED. THE
INTRICATE DETAIL IN
EACH OF THESE THREE
PIECES IS EVIDENCE OF
THE SKILL REQUIRED TO
CARVE SUCH ITEMS.
THE *HULU KRIS* ON THE
FACING PAGE, LEFT, IS
CALLED *HULU SEJUK* BY
THE KELANTANESE BUT
IS ALSO KNOWN AS *JAWA
DEMAM* AND WAS
ORIGINALLY A DESIGN
FROM PALEMBANG IN
SUMATRA. THE *HULU KRIS*
ON THE FACING PAGE,
RIGHT, IS KNOWN AS
HULU KRIS TAJONG, OR
PERKAKA (KINGFISHER)
AND IS DESIGNED TO BE
JABBED INTO AN
OPPONENT'S FACE. IT IS
OF KELANTAN MALAY
DESIGN, WITH INFLUENCE
FROM PATANI, SOUTHERN
THAILAND.
THIS PAGE SHOWS A
HULU KERDAS WHICH IS
BUGIS IN ORIGIN,
ALTHOUGH THIS
EXAMPLE WAS CARVED
IN KELANTAN
OR TERENGGANU.

WITH SUPPORT FROM
KRAFTANGAN, A QUASI-
GOVERNMENTAL AGENCY,
THESE YOUNG MEN ARE
UNDERGOING A COURSE
IN WOOD CARVING AT A
TRAINING CENTRE IN THE
TEMERLOH DISTRICT
OF PAHANG. THEIR WORK
IS DONE UNDER THE
GUIDANCE OF MASTER
CRAFTSMEN WHO
ARE GIVEN SPECIAL
ALLOWANCES AND SMALL
HONOURS TO COMPEN-
SATE THEM FOR THEIR
CONTRIBUTION. IN THIS
CASE THE STUDENTS
WERE PRIVILEGED TO
RECEIVE GUIDANCE FROM
TENGKU IBRAHIM
TENGKU WOK. THE
ENLIGHTENED POLICY
OF KRAFTANGAN IS
HELPING TO PRESERVE
TRADITIONAL SKILLS.

FACING PAGE, TOP:
THE LAST MALAY TIMBER
PALACE TO BE BUILT IN
MALAYSIA WAS SERI
MENANTI IN NEGRI
SEMBILAN. IT SERVED AS
THE RESIDENCE OF THE
YANG DI-PERTUAN BESAR,
TUANKU MUHAMMAD.
FACING PAGE, BOTTOM:
A MOSQUE OVER
300 YEARS OLD, MADE
FROM CHENGAL WOOD
AND ROOFED IN
TRADITIONAL *GENTING*,
OR HAND-MADE CLAY
TILES. ORIGINALLY IT WAS
SITED AT KAMPUNG LAUT,
A VILLAGE ACROSS THE
KELANTAN RIVER FROM
KOTA BAHRU. WHEN IT
APPEARED THAT THE
RIVER BANK MIGHT ERODE
AND COLLAPSE, TAKING
THE MOSQUE WITH IT,
THE BUILDING,
CONSTRUCTED WITHOUT
NAILS USING THE
TECHNIQUE OF *TEBUK-
PASAK*, OR MORTISE AND
TENON, WAS DISMANTLED
AND RECONSTRUCTED AT
ITS PRESENT SITE AT
NILAM PURI.
THIS PAGE: THIS
CLOSE-UP OF THE
DETAILS OF MASJID
KAMPUNG LAUT SHOWS
CLEARLY THE FLAT
CARVED RAILING OR
SOBEK. THE HANDMADE
CLAY ROOF TILES CAN
ALSO BE SEEN, AS WELL AS
THE UPCURVING ROOF
JOINT OR *PERABUNG*,
EVIDENCE OF THAI
INFLUENCE.

TEXTILES

Textile weaving in Malaysia has come a long way from its earliest roots. Originally working from homegrown and homespun materials, Malaysia's textile makers now prefer imported and commercially available cloths and threads. While various types of cotton are cultivated in Malaysia, the import of inexpensive European cotton goods at the beginning of the 19th century, together with a domestic preference for growing export crops, led to a decrease in local cotton production. Malaysia, like most Southeast Asian countries, still imports cotton, silk and metallic yarns for domestic use. The metallic threads come from Europe and China, while white cotton yarns have traditionally been from India. Bundles of two-ply silk threads used to come from China unbleached.

Older cloths are predominantly in the red-purple range of colours. Relatively few — mostly cotton cloths — are in tones of green and blue. Yellow cloths are even less common, mainly because use of that colour was reserved for the Malay rulers. Colours are usually seen to fall into two main categories — *muda* or light and *tua* or dark and rich; *tua* literally means 'old' or 'ripe'. The in-between shades are referred to in terms of the natural environment. Some of the traditional metaphorical colour names are *kulit langsat* or 'skin of the lansium fruit' for beige; *pinang masak*, 'ripe areca nut' for bright orange; *darah ikan*, 'blood of the fish' for blood red; *pucuk pisang*, 'banana leaf shoot' (pale green) and so forth.

The use of indigo hearkens back to an older tradition associated with the earliest cotton weaving. So important was indigo that at one time the locals even preferred to cultivate it rather than the spices of the archipelago, even though the latter was a trading item. An old method of indigo preparation consists of boiling the shoots, bark and twigs of the indigo plant in water. The dye in its concentrated pure state is stored in a lidded earthenware jar. A first dipping in a dyebath yields green, while subsequent steepings result in shades of blue, darkening eventually to black. Vegetable dyes can bind to a cloth by a process of simple oxidization, or together with some alkali such as wood ash or alum. Gypsum and lime are further added as mordants to the dye paste, giving it a silvery shine.

Reds are extracted from three main sources: *sepang* wood, *mengkudu* and a resin traditionally termed 'dragon's blood'. When shavings of the wood of the *sappan* tree are boiled in water, the resulting mixture dyes threads a vermilion red. Repeated dyeing gives a deep red with a slight yellow tint. *Mengkudu*, a brew of pulverised roots of the *morinda* tree, mixed with lime, yields shades of red and purplish red. The celebrated dragon's blood resin, which comes from Sumatra, the Malay Peninsula and Borneo, is yielded by the fruit of a climbing rattan which the Malays call *rotan jernang*. This resin is also used as a lacquer. Yellows were and still are obtained from tumeric roots.

Brewing vegetable dyes is a drawn-out process; it may take months to extract a dye and coax it to be absorbed by plant (or animal) fibres to the desired colour. Also, plants may need to be gathered during certain times of the year in order for the dyes extracted from them to be effective. If one were to ignore such romantic names as dragon's blood and consider the mess and stench of fermenting vegetation, it is easy to understand the attraction of modern synthetic dyes. The chemistry of dyes has been an exact science for years, and chemical dyes are often more fast to light than natural ones. In earlier centuries, when quick, simple yet efficient aniline dyes were not available, people spent time over and

PRECEDING PAGES:
STYLISED VEGETAL
MOTIFS ABOUND IN
WOVEN FABRICS.
FACING PAGE: A MODEL
WEARING THE TWO
TYPES OF WOVEN SILK
CLOTHS WHICH MADE UP
THE UNTAILORED
COSTUME OF CHE SITI
WAN KEMBANG, A
FORMER FEMALE RULER
OF KELANTAN. THE
BODICE WRAP IS OF
KAIN LIMAR AND HER
SARUNG OF SONGKET.
A HEAVY SONGKET
STOLE COVERS HER
BARE SHOULDERS.

above their household chores on dyeing yarns. The exercise was almost a ritual. The magic and mystery associated with the master dyers of old is in fact simply their knowledge of how to handle the natural materials around them — a knowledge culled from trial and error laced with spiritual inspiration.

LOOMS

The creation of textiles involves the process of weaving, which is interlacing parallel longitudinal threads, called warp, at right angles with horizontal threads called weft. The tool used to effect this process is the loom. There are several types of looms in Malaysia. The oldest and simplest is the body-tension loom. The longitudinal warp threads are threaded through two boards or beams, a breast beam and a warp beam. The former is held in place at the weaver's waist by being joined by a rope or string to a back strap made of a pad of wood, woven matting or leather placed at the back of the weaver; the latter is supported or braced by the feet of the weaver, who sits with legs stretched out. Thus, the position of the body keeps the warp threads taut. The weaver then moves a shuttle containing the weft threads back and forth through the warp.

The total length of the warp cannot exceed more than twice the distance from the waist to the feet of the weaver, which is about 160 cm long, while the width of the body-tension loom would be as wide as the arm span of the weaver, or between 60-80 cm. Such a foot-braced body-tension loom has a continuous warp so that the completed cloth is a cylindrical-shaped piece when removed from the loom. The cylindrical cloth is divided into two halves, one running from the weaver's feet to her waist, the other from the waist back to the feet, one above the other. These are called the upper and lower webs. A rectangular length of cloth is obtained by cutting the cylinder along the unwoven section of the warp, with the unwoven threads often left as fringes or tassels.

Another type of body-tension loom is where the warp is fixed to a house pillar, post, tree or some other support. Sitting on the ground or on a low stool, the weaver braces her feet against a piece of wood firmly fixed in the ground. The warp threads are inclined at an angle towards her and can be as long as two to three metres, or even longer. Such a loom takes up much space. Alternatively, the warp beam is fixed into an upright wooden frame instead of being attached to a post. In this type of loom the warp threads can be rolled up so that the loom takes up less space.

Frame looms differ from the body-tension loom in that a frame is used instead of the weaver's body to support and maintain the even tension of the warp. The loom now used by the Malays is a frame loom with the shuttle carrying the weft threads thrown by hand. The loom is an upright frame and is fitted with a device called a reed or comb to thread fine silk yarns. The frame allows the weaver freer movements compared to the strap and post type; also, wider cloths can be woven on this loom than on older back strap ones. For all ordinary cloths, two sets of heddles are used. A heddle is a series of vertical cords each having, in the middle, a loop through which a warp-thread passes. By adding more sets of heddles and more threads per heddle, the finished fabric can be coarser or have a particular texture and finish. Kelantan weavers, for example specialise in a textured fabric called *pantat siput*, or 'mussel's derriere'.

In the Malay context, over the centuries — in common with other master craftsmen — the most skilled weavers were employed by rulers and chiefs. Patrons employed weavers to make rich fabrics for their personal use or as gifts to be given to loyal subjects. Up till today, these fine textiles are treasured heirlooms and some even form part of the regalia of modern Malaysia's sultanates. Though scattered across the Peninsula, in West Malaysia the craft is concentrated in the two East Coast states of Kelantan and Terengganu. Kelantan's production is lesser, both in quantity and range, from Terengganu's. In Kelantan the majority of the looms are around the capital, Kota Bharu. Terengganu is acclaimed as the home of the finest work. Most of the intricate patterned cloths of the last century have emanated from this state. In the towns near Kuala Terengganu, the capital, are communities of weavers; every home here has a loom, while some have three or even four.

All stages of hand-woven cloth production done locally are usually carried out by women or young girls. Weaving at the level of a cottage industry is run by an entrepreneur, usually a woman, who may or may not be a weaver herself. She is something of a trader, collecting orders and distributing dyed yarns, beaters and shuttles to the weavers. If this entrepreneur is not a weaver herself, she hires a master-weaver to set up the warping frame and looms, or even to design weaving patterns. Actual weaving is done in the homes by weavers on their own looms, or on looms installed by the entrepreneur. The workers usually operate the looms in between chores.

When the loom is set for the weaver and the design already set with the threads of the warp arranged so that they form a repetitive pattern, all the weaver has to do is to follow it in the same colours. Such purely mechanical work is usually executed by young girls. The most productive years of a weaver are between ages twenty and thirty. Between thirty and forty, she is too occupied with running a large household; by fifty her eyesight begins to fail.

TYPES OF TEXTILES

Woven cloths: the Malay plaid

The plaid replaces earlier figurative patterns and decorative techniques. There are many varieties of plaid depending on the size of the squares, the colours used and the relationship between the colours of the warp and the weft. In these checked cloths, the warp is in two or more harmonising colours. An ordinary checked piece is the *corak Muar*, 'Muar pattern', which has a simple check pattern of broad squares in muted shades. Muar is a town in Johor state whose inhabitants used to prefer these large checked cloths woven in Terengganu. Thus, patterns are known by the name of their best markets. *Kain Pahang*, 'Pahang cloth' which has smaller squares, is named after the state of Pahang on the East Coast.

Another popular plaid is the *kain Bugis*, 'Bugis cloth', of which there are many varieties. The pattern is often an intricate network of small squares where several colours may be used; the background is usually green or red. The weft is usually in different yet harmonising colours. The checked design may be further divided into smaller units by thin lines of light colour. The square spaces created by the lines may have designs in gold and silver thread.

A COTTON GIN TO SEPARATE THE SEEDS FROM THE FIBRE. ALTHOUGH VARIOUS TYPES OF COTTON ARE CULTIVATED IN MALAYSIA, IT RELIES MORE ON IMPORTED COTTON YARNS FOR DOMESTIC USE.

Tie-and-dye: warp and weft ikat

Here, the individual threads of the warp and weft are the same colour throughout their length. Sometimes short lengths of the yarn are tied (in Malay, *ikat*) round with dye-proof strips of banana tree fibre and then immersed in the dye. The position of the bindings may be changed after two or three successive dyeings. The outlines of patterns created with such partially dyed yarns are slightly fuzzy or blurred. This effect is created because the edges of the bindings are never completely dye-proof, and dye seeps into the bound sections meant to resist it. The skilled weaver puts this effect to good use. A modern simplified technique is where sections of the warp are in fact painted with dye.

Iban women in Sarawak weave on a body-tension loom with a continuous warp. A blanket, called *pua*, is formed by stitching together side-by-side the two webs of the woven tube (which were originally joined end-to-end). In warp-ikat *pua*, the threads of the two webs have been tied together for the dyeing process, resulting in their having mirror-image patterns. If half a motif reaches the edge of a web, it is completed when the two webs are joined together. These blankets are usually fringed at both ends. This is because gaps were left in the weaving, at the two joints of the upper and lower webs. Woven *pua* terminate with one or two rows of coarse twining, so that the edges do not fray.

The import of silk yarns, and the local manufacture of silk later, marked a milestone in Malaysian textiles. To facilitate easier handling of the finer silk threads, a reed or comb was introduced for the warp threads to pass through. Associated with the use of silk is a technique called weft-ikat, and sets of patterns very different from the patterns of Iban warp-ikat. Weft-ikat is similar to the warp-ikat technique except that it is the weft threads which are patterned in the ikat method before weaving. The weaver interlaces the patterned weft threads with the plain warp threads on the loom. The height of weft-ikat weaving in Malaysia is expressed in a Malay courtly cloth, a silk fabric called *kain limar*. The background or field, termed *tanah* (literally 'earth' in Malay), on some Malay weft-ikat cloths still retains the stripes and bands of earlier times. Made from natural dyes, *limar* comes in shades of dark or purplish red. Less common are green and orange. Old texts mention that court dyers were expected to dye *limar* in at least five colours. But by the early 20th century *limar* production had dwindled, tailing off by the 1960's.

Supplementary wefts

Besides *ikat*, two other Iban decorative techniques are *sungkit* and *pilih*, both of which are supplementary wefts. The former means 'to sew' or 'to embroider' with a special type of flat bamboo needle, *cubang*, which is similar to a net-maker's needle but smaller. With the help of this needle, the supplementary weft is sewn or woven, usually between two wefts of the main cloth, effectively wrapping the main wefts. *Pilih* means 'to choose' or pick; in this case to pick out the warp threads to be passed over. The introduced supplementary wefts form patterns on top of the main weave.

The Kadazan are the largest indigenous group in Sabah. Their traditional woman's length of hand-woven skirt is coloured black and decorated with horizontal and vertical strips of multicoloured woven geometric designs. Today, these intricate bands, called *langkit*, have been largely replaced by appliqued

gold and silver braid. The Rungus, a sub-group of the Kadazan, continue to weave a cloth called *kain pudang*, which is an indigo-dyed black cotton of about 45 cm in width. Supplementary weft threads are added to the base weave to form triangular and zig-zag patterns. These bands may be further flanked by narrow stripes of orange and yellow. The woven *kain pudang* is made into skirts, bodice wraps and shawls. The Dusun people (sometimes called Lotud) weave a cloth which is very similar to *kain pudang*. It is also black but has red selvages decorated with bands of orange or white stripes. Bajau women weave on a very wide body-tension loom and their striped material is called *kain mogah*. The most famous Bajau textile is the *destar*, a square cotton head-cloth patterned in multicoloured supplementary wefts on a black ground.

Songket is cloth decorated with gold and silver thread and is the pride of the Malaysian weaving industry. Its output, however, is not as large as that of Malay plaid cloths. A simple traditional loom with treadle-operated heddles and hand-thrown shuttles is used. Almost always on a background of silk, songket is created from a supplementary weft of metallic threads. While the word songket is related to the word *sungkit*, which is weft wrapping, songket brocade is in fact composed by the *pilih* technique, with the supplementary weft 'floating' over the warp. Sometimes the introduced weft passes on top of as many as five consecutive warp threads, although it is more common to have three.

Bamboo sticks are inserted through the warp according to a plotted pattern and are lifted in a set sequence during the weaving process. Sometimes the pattern to be created with the supplementary metallic thread is tacked on to the warp with white cotton thread before the shed sticks are placed. For

less experienced weavers, motifs that are to be created during the weaving process are plotted on graph paper as a guiding sample; very experienced weavers, however, work from memory. The metallic thread, which starts at one end and doubles back and forth over and under the warps until the motif is formed, is then cut off. The thread is carefully twisted round those of the main cloth when the edges are reached to ensure firmness. When enough material for a complete *sarung* (a tubular skirt formed by joining the ends of a length of cloth) has been woven, a short length of the next *sarung* is done before the cloth is cut.

Because of its high quality gold threads, the best songket is not stiff. The threads can be unravelled and re-used when the silk base fabric has worn out. Due to the lavish use of metallic threads and the resulting weight, some *songket penuh*, ('full songket', where gold or silver threads cover the whole surface of the base cloth) have a combination of cotton warp and silk weft, allowing for a firmer foundation weave.

The Malays of coastal Sarawak also weave songket on a frame loom. Their songket are of two main types distinguished by the *kepala*, or 'head' panel. The less prestigious cloth has a floral panel *kepala*, while the *songket Brunei* — named after neighbouring Brunei — has a *tumpal* or *pucuk rebung* (bamboo shoot) pattern in the *kepala*, and is considered a full songket. Another name for this latter type is *jong sarat*, 'fully-laden junk'. A relatively modern songket has a plain field except for the border and is ornamented with motifs which are repeated and spaced out at intervals. A less costly variety uses threads, *benang*, of light grey or white silk to form the pattern instead of the gold or silver thread of the old songket; it is thus called *songket benang kilat* (*kilat* means shining). The patterning of this type of songket is much simpler, with regular geometric patterns and bands of parallel lines. Such a simplified pattern facilitates transfer onto a power loom.

Printed and painted cloths

Some woven cloths are further decorated with patterns stamped in gold leaf (*perada*). Plain cloths, dark coloured cloths, those with subdued designs or even the small checks of *kain Bugis* are used as bases. The material is usually calendered before gilding. The pattern is first stamped in gum arabic which has been applied on finely carved wooden blocks. While the glue is still wet, a gold leaf pattern of the same block is placed on it. The motifs of these gluework cloths are almost always floral, often a rosette or flower. In Java and Bali, these gilded cloths are called *kain perada;* in Malaysia, it is called *kain telipuk.* A modern and modified version is where paint of bronze or aluminium colour is applied by means of a stencil or brush to the cloth, often to coloured satin.

Pelangi is the tie-and-dye technique applied onto finished cloth instead of unwoven threads. Areas to be left undyed are tied, sewn or wrapped up tightly, so that the dye cannot penetrate. Random abstract shapes can be created in this way, but the Malay practice is to use floral scrolls or geometric designs. These designs are often first stamped in water-soluble red ferruginous earth on the cloth, the earth washing away during dyeing. The edges of the designs made by the wooden stamp are stitched tight so that the cloth puckers and the stitched area of the pattern protrudes as nodules. These nodules or pockets of cloth are bound with thread or with banana leaf or tree fibres before the cloth is immersed in a dyebath. The white areas of the cloth which had resisted the dye may later be coloured by hand. Earlier *pelangi* were often embellished with a border of *biku perak,* silver-thread lace of European import.

Insofar as the principle of batik is resisting the dye, it is similar to *limar* and *pelangi.* The resist method in batik, like *pelangi,* is carried out on already woven cloth. The word batik is derived from two words: the Javanese word *amba,* 'to write' and the Malay word for dot, *titik.* Thus *ambatik,* shortened to batik, means 'to write dots'. Patterns are drawn in wax on the cloth by means of a *canting,* a metal stylus with a reservoir for molten wax, or stamped in wax with blocks carrying patterns.

The labour-intensive stylus method as practised in Java was never popular in Malaysia, even from the earliest years of the industry here, in 1920's Kelantan. The block method, *cap* ('chop', or stamp) was adopted in Malaysia at the same time that it gained ground in Java. The earliest batik made of repeated patterns stamped out using wooden blocks was known as *kain pukul,* 'stamped cloth'. As the people of Kedah were the most avid consumers of this cloth, it was also called *kain batik Kedah.* Sometimes the background cloth was dyed while parts of the pattern were painted in by hand. After an initial import of copper blocks from Java, subsequent brass and tin ones were modelled locally. The *pekalongan* bouquet of Java's north coast came to Kota Bharu in 1948 and the batik industry was revived. The outline of the floral spray was composed by stamping several blocks in wax outline and filling the colours in by hand. In Terengganu in the 1950's, *sarung* in the style of Lasem (also on Java's north coast) were popular; such *sarung* of cream-coloured backgrounds supported creeping vines flanking a *kepala* filled with *pucuk rebung.* Sometimes, when a hand-drawn design was transferred to blocks, it was reduced, as was the case when the large cloud and rock patterns of Cirebon, in Java, were adopted in Malaysia. Again, Kelantan and Terengganu lead in batik production, although Kelantan outstrips the latter in this area.

More commercially-oriented production of batik by the metre also uses the discharge method. The cloth is dyed a dark colour and the outlines of the motif registered in wax applied by metal blocks. The colour is removed by dipping the cloth in an acid bleach solution. Pastel shade batik was first created this way. In discharge batik the outline of the pattern stands out more prominently.

Larger batik factories transformed the batik process, replacing the blocked wax with screen printing techniques, beginning with one colour on white cotton. In this process, the cloth is stretched out on a frame of the same size as the stencil. The cloth is positioned below the framed muslin stencil and the dye rubbed swiftly with a roller across the framed screen; the blocked-out areas of the screen resist the dye. One stencil is required for each colour. This time-saving process produces many more *sarung* in a given time than stamping or hand-drawing a resisting wax. A later development in this method was to add a layer of wax to obtain the crack lines characteristic of traditional wax-drawn batik.

By the 1960's a Malaysian style of batik emerged, as batikkers deliberately abandoned Javanese-influenced designs. New motifs were tried out, and a new hand-drawn batik evolved, characterised by the use of the *canting* to outline the design with a fine wax line, and a spread of flat colour covering large areas. An important new element was the addition of shading and dimension, achieved by blending shades and hues. Applying colours by hand this way is termed *conteng*, literally 'doodling'. This new style may be considered fabric painting as much as (or more than) batik. As an alternative to immersing the cloth in a dyebath, colours are applied with brushes. This experiment into creating new batik types was first known as alpha batik. Cloths used were voile, silk and cotton lawn, not for the traditional *sarung* but for batik by the metre. By the 1970's, batik for the tourist market became a new motivation. This type of batik goes through very simplified processes and the patterns are much less complicated. Colour schemes are muted and very often monochromatic.

The Malaysian definition of batik thus acquired a much larger meaning than the Javanese one of resist-dyeing with laborious *canting*-drawn wax lines or stamps. Today, batik in Malaysia has come to be defined by certain design styles and sensibilities, and by the high percentage of floral motifs, more than the process used. At the same time, batik has became more than a Malay cloth; it is a Malaysian cloth. With diminishing aristocratic patronage and the transformations of a modern economy, textile producers have evolved a viable industry along modern lines, free of older traditions and using labour-saving mass production techniques up to and including photographic printing. The old system of anonymous artisans is giving way before a new style and organisation of the industry that stresses individual talents and promotes recognised batik artists and designers. In a further development, Terengganu recently produced Malaysia's first pure silk batik from locally manufactured silk.

EMBROIDERY

Embroidery is a quicker and less costly means of decorating textiles compared to *limar*, *telipuk* and songket. Malay embroidery, *sulam*, uses gold paper appliqué and metallic threads in groups of three or five strands couched down with small stitches of coloured threads. Sometimes the satin stitch is

used, especially in a particular type of embroidery called *tekat*, where templates shaped from layers of paper are completely covered in raised relief (refer to page 139 for a lengthier treatment of *tekat* embroidery). Appliqué work includes the use of mica or mirror chips. Generally, the peoples of Sarawak and Sabah include beads and shells in their appliqué work.

PATTERNS AND MOTIFS

Iban patterns in weaving vary from the naturalistic, (or as naturalistic as can be achieved within the limits of the threads crossed at right angles), to designs so abstract that only the weaver knows what they really represent. Through many generations, the meanings of motifs have altered slightly; two weavers may interpret a given design differently. Woven motifs which symbolised an event, thought or even a dream have become through time only designs with names and by now simply impersonal ornamentation. Iban designs were the property of the individual weaver and were handed down from mother to daughter. Generally, human figures represent ancestors or deities. In design layout, a creeper pattern usually joins varying forms into a coherent whole (refer to page 151 for a more detailed treatment of Iban textiles). People in Sabah prefer to decorate their cloths in stripes and geometrics.

Awan larat means 'protracted' or 'trailing' clouds (*awan*) and is the Malay arabesque. Swirling cloud formations are evocative and conjure up variations of the S-scroll in the artist's mind. These curves pervade Malay art. The tendrils, vines and foliated creepers are in fact variations of the basic circle.

An unsewn rectangular cloth called *kain lepas*, 'unfettered cloth', would inevitably have as borders on the two shorter ends, called *punca* (beginning), a row of isosceles triangles variously referred to as *pucuk rebung* (bamboo shoot) in the Peninsula and Sumatra, and *tumpal* elsewhere in Indonesia. For a *sarung*, the *kepala* almost always is filled with two confronting rows of these triangles. In a further elaboration, the triangle is trimmed with ornate feathery edges and becomes the plume of the strutting cockerel. This latter is the *lawi ayam*, 'cockerel's plume', forming the borders or special panels of Malay silks and brocades. Less common is the duck's tail, *lawi itek*, which is broader and shorter.

The interlocked chevrons and diamond grid forming overall patterns of fields are an interplay of geometric forms. Many *kain limar* and songket are patterned thus. The spaces enclosed by these overall patterns are usually filled with stylised florals which are often eight-pointed. Such a continuous ornate pattern is called *teluk berantai*, 'linked or interlocking bays'.

USES OF TEXTILES

Malays use the word *kain* to refer to textiles in general and the *sarung* in particular. The *sarung* has a *badan* or body, a specially decorated panel called *kepala*, 'head', and *tepi*, 'edges' or 'borders'. A woven rectangular piece is often used as a garment in itself. These untailored garments are folded, draped, wrapped and tied in various styles. One does not merely *pakai kain*, 'wear clothes', but one *ikat kain*, 'ties cloths' (round oneself). The versatile *sarung* can be used in a variety of ways: as a shroud, as a head wrap for protection from the sun or as a cloth for bathing. Large pieces of fabric are used as partitions and as sleeping tents.

AN IBAN WEARING A HAND-WOVEN *BAJU ARA*, AN IKAT JACKET WITH A REPETITIVE MOTIF OF CHEQUERED STRIPES CALLED *EMPETUT*, IN IMITATION OF THE COLOURS OF A SNAKE OF THE SAME NAME FOUND IN BORNEO (*NATRIX TROPIDONOTUS*). THE HEM IS DECORATED WITH BEADS OF ALTERNATING COLOURS, SHAPES AND SIZES.

Textiles are also used in ceremonies and rituals. During an important rite-of-passage, like a wedding, a ritually ornamented bed is usually hung with precious textiles and decorated with embroidered cushions. Decorative panels for ends of ceremonial pillows and bolsters, called *muka bantal*, are filled with *sulam*. These panels in pairs come mostly in rectangular or circular shapes; the latter sometimes have scalloped edges. Hexagonal and octagonal ones are less common. The *tekat* technique is still popular on the Peninsula and is often applied to the surfaces of three-dimensional objects.

Just as Malay embroidery is most often used for wedding ceremonies, full songket has become the attire of bridal couples. High quality songket pieces were traditionally kept as family heirlooms handed down through the generations, and used to be part of the bride price. *Kain songket* continues to be produced today in standard *sarung* lengths of 100 cm by 180 cm. The cloth is favoured for social occasions, while its use in ceremonies, especially weddings, ensures its popularity. Sets of songket for the bridal couple can be hired for the occasion from a *mak andam* (mistress of wedding ceremonies).

A pre-wedding ceremony also uses embroidered textiles. This is the *tikar akad nikar* (in Malay, *tikar* means 'mat' and *akad nikar* 'promise of marriage', i.e. engagement). Squares of different sizes called *delamak* are meant to cover and decorate conical food covers (*tudung saji*) woven from *pandanus* leaves. These embroidered squares are only meant for ceremonial use.

Some of the warp-ikat *pua* of the Iban are for special religious purposes. The *pua kumbu* are used for defining sacred space when they are hung up to surround an area where a ceremony is to be performed. As women's creative products, textiles are often associated with fertility and are used as protective coverings, in rice cultivation rituals and for rites-of-passage.

THE FUTURE

Change in the pattern of life is causing many handicraft skills to become lost arts. These skills are the product of a group, not the possession of an individual. Yet individual creativity and fashion are valued differently at different times. In the case of batik, for example, designers' names have emerged from the mass of nameless artisans. Interaction between the preservation of ancient practices and innovations has resulted in a very wide range of cloth forms and functions in this country. Traditional crafts have always been part of intimate family or close-knit community activities.

An impersonal and expansive approach to preserving crafts will inevitably demand intelligent, sustained and concerted effort. At the same time an artificial preservation of hybrid horrors cannot be acceptable. While subtleties of taste and style cannot be easily imparted, the basic qualities are obvious: dyes should not run or fade, yarns must be of reasonable strength, and ultimately the hand-crafted textile must be superior to a similar one produced by machine.

Khoo Joo Ee

A CONTEMPORARY SUPPLEMENTARY WEFT SKIRT WOVEN BY MESSINIE ANAK PENGHULU ADONG OF ULU SEBUYAU (AHLI SARAKUP INDU DAYAK SARAWAK). TWO TYPES OF GOLD SUPPLEMENTARY WEFT THREADS ARE CONTINUOUSLY PATTERNED ALONG A BRIGHT COTTON RED WARP BACKGROUND TO CREATE A BOLD DESIGN CALLED *MATA ARI* (THE SUN).

THIS PAGE: THE WOVEN MALAY PLAID WORN BY MEN AS HEAD-CLOTHS, SHIRTS AND JACKETS, ANKLE-LENGTH *SARUNG* OR WAIST-TO-KNEE LENGTH WRAPS (*SAMPING*) OVER LONG TROUSERS. THESE CHECKERED *PELEKAT* WERE ALSO MADE INTO TROUSERS. SOME OF THE CLOTHS APPEAR TO BE CALENDARED OR OF SILK. FACING PAGE: PICTURE SHOWS THE SPECIAL PANEL, THE *KEPALA*, WHICH STANDS OUT FROM THE REST OF THE *SARUNG*. FOLLOWING PAGES: THE *KEPALA* OF A *SARUNG* AS THE VISUAL CENTRE IS ELABORATELY WOVEN IN AN OLDER PIECE OF *SARUNG*. THE STANDARD MOTIF IS TWO ROWS OF CONFRONTING ISOSCELES TRIANGLES, WHICH IN TURN ARE FLANKED BY BORDERS, LYING HORIZONTALLY WITH THEIR APEXES TOWARDS THE CENTRE. THESE TRIANGLES ARE POETICALLY CALLED COCKEREL'S PLUMES OR *LAWI AYAM*.

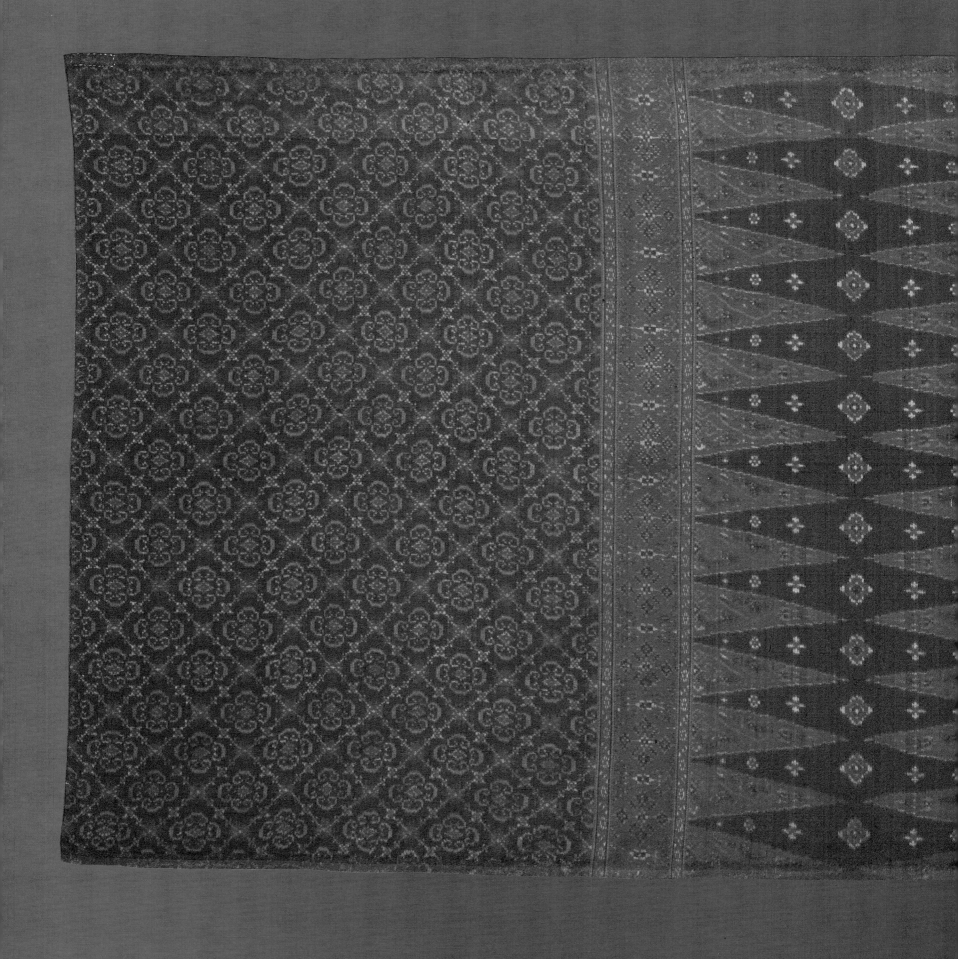

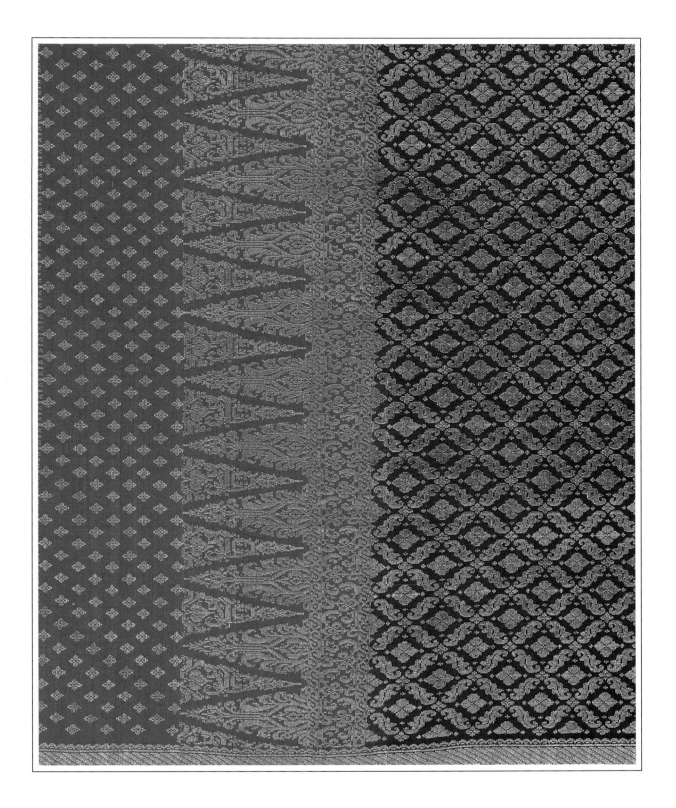

BOTH SONGKET
PIECES HAVE THE CLASSIC
TRIANGULAR MOTIF IN
THEIR SPECIAL PANELS OF
BACKGROUND COLOURS
WHICH CONTRASTS WITH
THE FIELD, AND THE
INTERLOCKING LOZENGE,
TELUK BERANTAI
('CHAINED BAYS') DESIGN,
AS THEIR FIELDS. THE
DECORATIVE PANELS ARE
SO FILLED WITH THE
METALLIC 'FLOATING'
THREADS AS TO
ALMOST COVER THE BASE
MATERIAL. SUCH OLDER
PIECES DISPLAY
TYPICALLY ELABORATE
PATTERNING.

A YOUNG WEAVER AT
THE LOOM. THE ART OF
WEAVING, STILL VERY
MUCH A COTTAGE
INDUSTRY, IS LARGELY
CONFINED TO EAST
MALAYSIA AND THE EAST
COAST STATES OF THE
PENINSULA, WHERE IT IS
EXECUTED ON THE
MALAY FRAME LOOM.

THIS PAGE: AN
INGENIOUS WAY TO
CARRY A BABY — WITH A
SARUNG AS A SLING. THE
LENGTH OF CLOTH IS
OPENED OUT AS A SEAT
FOR THE CHILD.

FACING PAGE: AN EARLY
HISTORICAL BATIK *CAP*,
OR STAMPED DESIGN.
THE *KEPALA* OF THE
SARUNG FEATURES THE
ENDEARING TRIANGULAR
PUCUK REBUNG (BAMBOO
SHOOT) MOTIF. THE
FLOWERS-IN-A-BASKET
MOTIF BETRAYS
FOREIGN INFLUENCE.

IN RELATIVELY MODERN
BATIK PRODUCTION,
TOUCHING UP OF THE
DESIGN IS MANUALLY
DONE WITH A BRUSH
AFTER THE PATTERNS ON
THE CLOTH HAVE BEEN
BLOCK PRINTED.

THE TRADITIONAL
WAY OF REMOVING THE
WAX FROM THE PRINTED
BATIK IS BY BOILING.
COTTON, A STURDIER
MATERIAL THAN
NATURAL SILK, CAN
BETTER WITHSTAND
REPEATED DYEING
AND BOILING.

DYED AND PRINTED
LENGTHS OF BATIK,
MOSTLY OF COTTON OR
COTTON VOILE, ARE
HUNG OUT IN THE
COMPOUND OF BATIK
FACTORIES TO DRY. THE
BRILLIANT COLOURS
SUGGEST THE USE OF
ANILINE DYES.

MALAYSIA'S SILK
BATIK IS VERY OFTEN
HAND-PAINTED, AN ART
WHICH IS A MODERN
BREAKAWAY FROM
THE OLDER METHOD
OF USING THE *CANTING*
TO TRACE OUT AND
FILL IN DESIGNS WITH
WAX, LEAVING THE
APPLICATION OF
COLOUR TO FULL-
IMMERSION DYEING

THE ART OF EMBROIDERY

by Siti Zainon Ismail

The embroidery of gold thread by Malay women is an age-old art. The use of embroidered adornments is often depicted and mentioned in classical Malay literary texts. For example, in the *Salasilah Melayu dan Bugis*, the chief attendant of the palace is described "wearing a brilliant shawl of yellow silk embroidered with the flowers of the angsana". Embroidery is also mentioned in the *Hikayat Inderaputera*, which describes "…the palace (as) furnished with mattresses decorated in a figured golden fabric and embroidery featuring swirling floral designs on subtle patterned chintz". Raja Chulan made reference to embroidery in the *Misa Melayu*: "unfurled at the top was a drape adorned with interlaced floral motifs heavily embroidered in gold thread, adding richness and splendour to the patterned velvet fabric".

In *tekat* embroidery, gold thread is embroidered on a base fabric of velvet. This combination is also known as *suji timbul* (raised or embossed embroidery) or *tekat bersuji*. The term *suji* is also often associated with embroidery done with silk thread. In classical Malay texts, the embroidered pieces are referred to as *dewangga baldu beremas* (velvet patterned or embroidered with gold). In short, the terms 'sulam', 'tekat' and 'suji' are used interchangeably to refer to embroidery, but embroidery with at least one of the following characteristics: needlework in relief, raised from the surface of the fabric with the embroidery threads sewn over a filling; thickset layers of gold threads pressed closely together and anchored to the base cloth by lighter threads; or an embroidery-appliqué (*kelingkan*) which fixes gold leaf to the surface of the cloth.

The origins of these types of Malay embroidery are uncertain. Based on the use of gold thread, and on similarities of appearance and form, one could suppose that they began together with the weaving of songket. Traditional embroidery of the Malay world includes royal paraphernalia of the istana (palace), regalia and ornaments embellishing the throne and royal bridal dais, for royal weddings and coronations. Windstedt saw in this a connection to the luxurious and prestigious textiles and embroideries of India and China: "The invariable use of embroidered cloths at court, as well as the Sanskrit name of the curtain fringe, probably points to an Indian origin for the art; and the Chinese chronicles of the 10th century speak of 'flowered silk adorned with pearls', and 'canopies of feathers and embroidered curtains' ".

Embroidery is often associated with the garments of royalty. Court costumes for men and women were richly encrusted with stitchery worked in silk, gold and silver threads, often studded with glittering and ornate embellishments. The clothes worn by Anggun Cik Tunggal — a famous character in one of the legends in the pantheon of Malay folklore — are described as being brocaded with glass spangles (see *Hikayat Anggun Cik Tunggal*): "Glass by the thousands at his waist, glass by the hundreds at his feet, strung together in a suit of diamonds". What is referred to here as 'glass' is the glitter of spangles sewn or embroidered on the accessory worn around the waist (a belt, girdle or cummerbund) or on the pants or trousers. The scintillating brilliance is produced by small, sparkling decorative sequins 'labuci', 'jemeki' or spangles or gold thread covered with metallic speckles. The use of such materials points to Chinese influence. Such gold thread embroidery, complemented by glass beads or sequins, is still made.

FACING PAGE: A TRADITIONAL SUMATRAN WEDDING FAN WORKED IN GOLD THREAD AND DECKED WITH BEADS AND SPANGLES. THE BASE MATERIAL IS OF YELLOW VELVET AND IS FRINGED WITH GOLD-COLOURED LACE. THE PADDED COUCHING SEEN IN THIS PIECE EXEMPLIFIES THE RELIEF EFFECT OF *TEKAT* NEEDLEWORK, WHICH HAS BECOME A TRADEMARK OF MALAY EMBROIDERY.

Like other crafts, embroidery was not practised in isolation. The opening of new trade routes between the Malay Archipelago and China, refinement in the field of art and aesthetic appreciation as well as the flowering of all the arts and crafts, resulted in an exchange of decorative styles, materials and techniques. During the golden age of Malay rule in Melaka, gold thread embroidery in China greatly inspired local craftsmen and women. Numerous items of Chinese embroidery found their way into Melaka, some as gifts from the Chinese emperor to the sultans of Melaka. The texts record the Chinese emperor sending the sultans "velvets, silks and gauzes embroidered with gold", as well as the famous silken embroidered dragon robes. In the 16th century the forms, designs and techniques which craftsmen had imbibed from China continued to blossom throughout the country, in the new courts that arose after Melaka's fall to the Portuguese in 1511.

In the context of old court tradition, clothes embroidered with gold thread and sequins are strictly forbidden to commoners. The basic materials used for embroidery — velvet and gold thread — were regarded as exclusive possessions of the privileged and wealthy, and ordinary subjects were permitted to wear them only if they were bestowed as gifts from the king.

Centres for embroidery flourished in Perak, Johor and Pahang. In Perak and Pahang, the art of embroidery is believed to have been fostered in the palace in Kuala Kangsar, Perak; in Pekan in Pahang; and Kota Tinggi and Keluang in Johor. The heritage of gold and silver thread embroidery as a traditional craft in Melaka was chronicled in 1880 by Ambrose B. Rathborne: "The women are clever at embroidery, especially with silver and gold threads..."

In the late 19th century, gold paper appliqué was popular among the Malay community in southern Johor and the Johor-Riau region. This type of work (known as *tekat kelingkan*) was thought by British scholars to have been inspired directly by the work coming from India and China, though the motifs and designs of this form are clearly more Arab in inspiration. Gold thread embroidery was popular in Perak and in Klang in Selangor. Indeed, the Malays of Sarawak were well-known at this time for both songket and embroidery work.

THE CRAFT TODAY

The technique of embroidering gold thread in relief is still practised today in Perak and Selangor. In the states of Kelantan and Terengganu, the art of embroidery involves the use of gold paper appliquéd on to velvet or silk. In Sabah in East Malaysia, particularly among the Bajau-Irranun people, gold thread embroidery is interlaced with layers of multicoloured threads, whereas the Malay-Bruneians in Sabah practise another variation of this type of needlework.

Embroidery is also done with various other materials. For example, Sarawakian embroidery uses decorative stitches of thread made of gold paper (known as *tekat benang kelingkan* or *keringkam Sarawak*). *Terekam Terengganu* uses a pure gold filament, thicker than other varieties of fine gold thread and worked on silk or georgette to make various traditional headgear such as scarves or stoles (*selendang*), and veils (*selayah*) in Sarawak or *manto* (small stole) in Johor-Riau.

In Perak, the art of embroidery was originally monopolised by royalty. The Raja Permaisuri of Perak (Permaisuri Sultan Idris Murshi du A'dzam Shah, 1887-1906) was not only a designer of decorative stitching but a prolific embroiderer herself. A British contemporary, Leonard Wray, describing the work of gold thread embroidery of that time, pays tribute to Her Highness' craftsmanship: "The beautiful embroidery was designed and worked by H.H. the Raja Permaisuri, the second wife of the Sultan of Perak… These were the presents which the Sultan of Perak gave to H.R.H. the Prince and Princess of Wales when they visited Singapore in 1901. The Raja Permaisuri is acknowledged to be one of the most artistic designers and workers in the country…"

Perhaps the best example of her creation at its most sumptuous is the ceremonial attire of Sultan Abdullah Muhammad Syah II, the 26th sultan who ruled Perak from 1874 to 1876. It is a resplendent outfit adorned with gold-thread embroidery of fern- and dagger-shaped motifs. Worked on white fabric, it combined regular counted thread filling stitches and the swirling floral designs characteristic of many other creations of 19th century Malay embroidery.

Other embroidery works produced by the Raja Permaisuri of Perak included a square covering for the royal dais, prayer mats, numerous intricate and multicoloured tapestries, bolsters, crochetted pillows, kris sheaths, cushion covers, kris holders and decorative or ornamental boxes. She was also known to have used her fine craftsmanship to make other traditional royal paraphernalia such as the *ciu* or *cior*, a special three-layered mat or divan embellished with gold or silver embroidery, and meant for the sultan.

Though it is still an integral part of royal pomp, splendour and ceremony, the art of embroidery has since spread beyond the preserve of royalty and is now enjoyed by the common people, who practise the craft in their free time. Due to the meticulous and time-consuming nature of the work, embroidery is done only in stages, and only when required for a special purpose. Young ladies who are preparing for their wedding will work on their own trousseaux, making decorations for the bridal dais, the mosquito net and awning (*kelambu*) suspended over their matrimonial beds, curtains, door valances, pillow cases, decorative pillow-end plates, bedspreads, hand-held fans, betel sets (*tepak sirih*), food covers (*tudung saji*), shoes and many other ceremonial objects.

Embroidery is almost always limited to decorating functional articles, like clothing or furnishings. Embroidered pieces are used as decorations in special rites and ceremonies, such as during a wedding, a marriage proposal, the birth of a child, circumcision and the ceremony upon completion of one's reading of the Quran (*berkhatam Quran*), to name a few. Because the basic materials used in embroidery are costly, its use among the local people is rather restricted. Great care and attention is also required to maintain and preserve an embroidered item of fine workmanship and delicate elegance, and this makes *tekat* pieces impractical for everyday use.

A number of surviving embroiderers skilled in the art still deal directly with the Malaysian royal courts and palaces. They receive special commissions to work on embroidery pieces for official ceremonies at the istana, or even for the day-to-day needs of their royal patrons. In the state of Perak, for instance, embroidery as a handicraft is still very popular. The centres for Malay embroidery in

AN EMBROIDERED DECORATIVE TRAY COVER USING GOLD LEAF ON PAPER APPLIQUÉD ONTO VELVET, KNOWN AS *TEKAT KELINGKAN*. THE SIX-PETALLED FLOWER MOTIF ARRANGED IN SPRAWLING FORMATION (*SUSUN SULUR BAYUNG*) IS WORKED IN GOLD THREAD AND SPANGLES OVER PINK VELVET.

Perak are in Kuala Kangsar, Sayong, Kota Lama Kanan, Kota Lama Kiri, Kampong Belanja and Kampung Sadang in Parit, and Teluk Intan. Several areas in Kelang and Jugra in Selangor are also well-known for their magnificent embroidery and traditional fine craftsmanship.

THE PROCESS

The most important basic materials for embroidery are gold thread, white thread and velvet. Apart from these, other secondary materials like *sega* rattan, thick paper and starch (as adhesive) are used to make the template, the padding or filling that produces the 'raised effect' which — as some traditional practitioners of Malay embroidery would insist — is what the term *seni tekat* really refers to.

Base fabrics are usually a material like velvet, lustrous and with a short pile. The velvet is usually of a deep colour — ruby-red, burgundy or maroon, or purple, forest green or black. Light colours are sometimes used to create effective contrasts. The use of velvet distinguishes the embroidery of the Malays from that of the Peranakan or Straits-born Chinese of Penang and Melaka, who prefer silk or muslin. The backing fabric, put on before the actual emboidery takes place, is usually made from cotton or chintz placed in the centre of the stretcher frame (*pemidang*).

Sega (*Calamus caesius*) is a type of smooth shiny rattan with a polished finish. It is used to make the template or filling for the embroidery. The *sega* is cut according to the pattern that is to be produced. *Sega* is also used to reinforce or strengthen delicate work, for example the coilings around the edges of a food cover. Thick paper or several layers of ordinary paper glued together with starch or other adhesives can also be used to make up the backing for the embroidery. Many embroiderers prefer paper as the template because it is softer, more pliable and easier to cut to shape and paste onto the fabric. Coarser threads and other fibres can be used as fillings for very delicate work.

Wooden stretcher frames with or without legs or floorstands are constructed according to the dimensions of the work to be produced. The embroidery needle (known as *cubang* or *laulai*) is a medium-sized stylus used to twine the gold thread. This medium-sized stylus is made of bamboo strips measuring approximately 20 cm by 8 cm. The two bamboo strips are crossed together and tied like a crucifix. Strands of gold thread are wrapped over the point where the two bamboo pieces intersect. The stylus for embroidery can also be made of wood, copper, silver or animal horns.

STITCHING AND NEEDLEWORK

The gold thread from the stylus is stitched across the template or backing material from right to left. The method is somewhat akin to a technique known as underside couching, in which the fine thread used to hold the thicker couched gold thread is pulled with each stitch, thus bringing the couched gold thread down to the underside of the fabric at that point. From the front none of the couching stitches are visible, and the gold threads look as if they are sewn through the fabric. When the gold thread has been securely stitched to the template, it is fixed to the velvet with tiny stitches. The white thread has to go through the underside of the template without leaving any stitch mark on the surface. The joining

FACING PAGE, TOP:
THE TECHNIQUE OF
EMBROIDERING GOLD
THREAD OVER *MEMPULUR*.
THE FINISHED PRODUCT
ADORNS ORNAMENTAL
OBJECTS LIKE THIS
BRIDAL PILLOW (FACING
PAGE, BOTTOM), AND THE
LADY'S SLIPPERS ABOVE.

stitches must be tight and secure. The gold thread has to be placed closely together each time it is laid across the template so that no part of the template shows through. This gives the embroidery a fine, beautiful finish with precise outlines. The embroidery is worked over the entire motif until the template is covered with stitches. Sequins and beads are usually used to cover thread joinings or the empty spaces created by broken pieces of the template, which usually occur at the joints of stalks of flower motifs.

DESIGNS AND MOTIFS

The embroidery of the Straits-born Chinese generally employs animal and bird motifs, whereas Malay designs predominantly feature plant and floral motifs, calligraphic patterns and some stylised and geometric bird designs, usually arranged within interlacing patterns of coiling stems. Regardless of which motif is used to design Malay embroidery, all of them are organically-styled. The thickness and width of the template will determine the stitches employed.

Popular plant motifs used include the *pucuk paku* (a type of fern), bitter gourd leaf (*daun peria*), yam leaf (*daun keladi*), padi leaf or grain and bamboo shoots (*pucuk rebung*). The repertoire of flower designs used include the four-petalled clove blossom, the six-petalled mace or areca nut bloom, the five-petalled hibiscus, the sunflower, orchid, *bunga asam batu*, *bunga tongkeng* (a type of climbing plant, *Telosma cordata*), bitter gourd bud, white *cempaka*, chrysanthemum and the pomegranate flower.

Geometric designs include reticulated triangular and square patterns, checkerboard, lattice and plaited patterns, rectilineal lines or Dongson-like S- and double S shapes. Bird motifs are rare compared to plant and flower motifs. Of the several samplers of embroidery on display in the Muzium Negara in Kuala Lumpur, only one embroidered mat uses bird patterns as its primary motif. Bird motifs used in Malay embroidery have been modified to create the *awan larat* or 'continuous floating clouds' effect, in which the bird designs are interlinked with plant and flower motifs to form a composite design. Meanwhile in Sabah, calligraphic embroideries featuring the words 'Allah' and (Prophet) 'Muhammad' have been known to adorn the hangings or drapes of bridal platforms.

LAYOUT AND ARRANGEMENT OF MOTIFS

Motifs are combined in a harmonious arrangement. Geometric patterns and foliage motifs mingle gracefully in Malay embroidery works. For example in a door valance, plant motifs and geometric patterns like the swastika — two designs which would normally be incompatible with each other — are integrated, with the sharp, strident geometric lines muted by the organically-styled curves of the plant motifs. Similarly, triangular patterns are frequently arranged in tandem with plant motifs, either as a composite motif or as decorative borders in the *pucuk rebung* design. Here, the basic triangular patterns give a geometric feel while foliage details create flowing curves.

There are three types of layouts in which the motifs can be arranged: in single formation (*susun tunggal*), in crockets or sprawling formation (*susun sulur bayung*) and the intertwining formation known as *susun awan larat*. In the single formation layout the leaf, bud, blossom and stem in a flower motif are

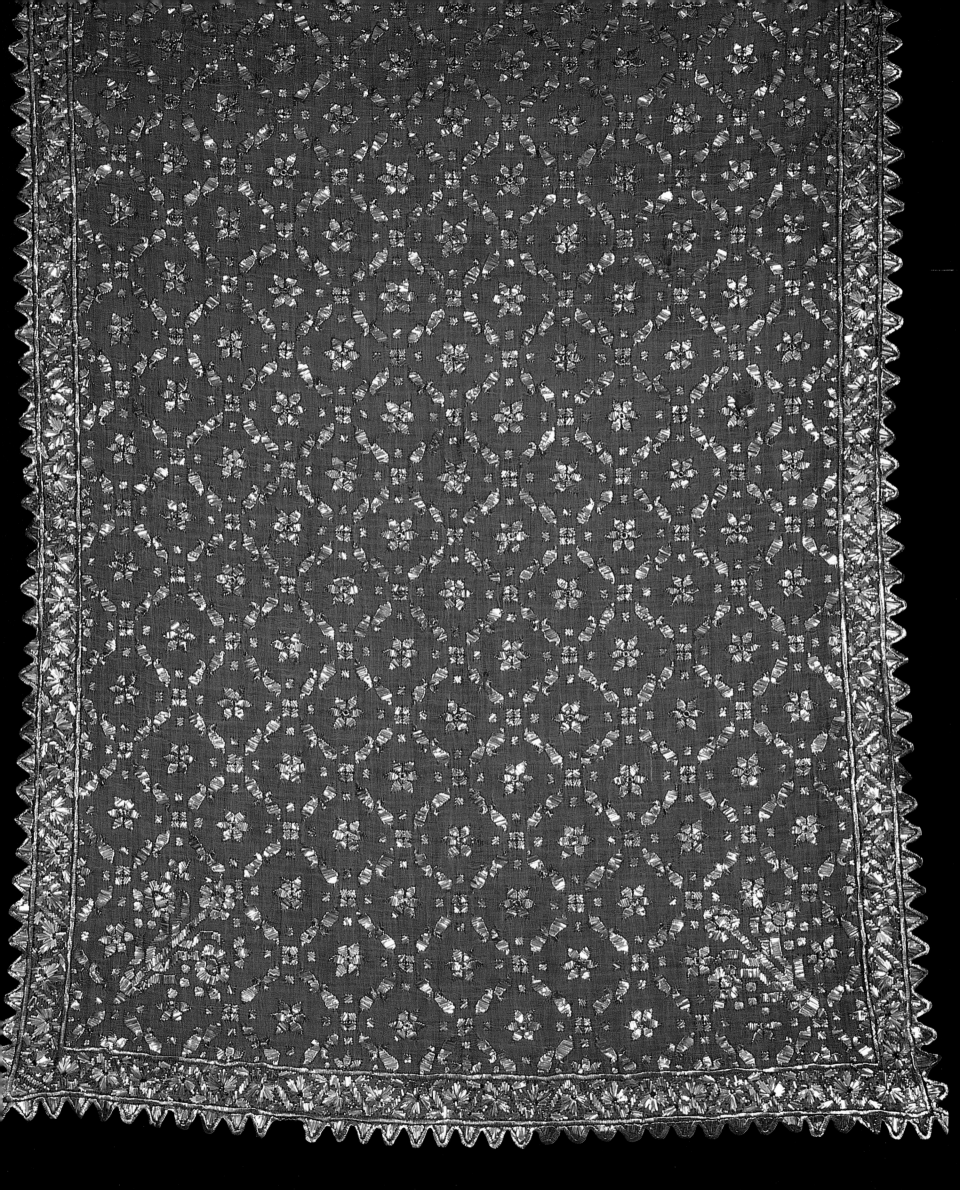

combined to form one whole 'flower stalk'. This type of arrangement is normally used for embroidery on square or rectangular surfaces, like cushions or pillow cases. In the crocket arrangement, the motifs are arranged in sprawling formation akin to the creeping and spreading tendrils of a plant. Flowers, leaves and shoots can also appear, but what is important is that each stem, stalk and leaf must be arranged symmetrically. For example, if a flower is placed in the centre of the design area, it must be flanked on its right and left with leaves, tendrils or creepers which unfurl and twist upwards and downwards to give the design a sense of balance, proportion and congruity. Embroidery works which often have motifs arranged in this type of formation include door valances, the thresholds of the bridal dais (*bendul pelamin*) and the five- or seven-layered multicoloured embroidery designed *peterana* (platform) or *tikar panca* (marriage mat).

Motifs arranged in the intertwining formation of *awan larat* usually cover the entire design area. The pattern is interconnected in such a way that it is almost impossible to trace where the embroidery or stitchwork begins. It is because of the difficulty of discerning the representations of flowers and other natural objects which make up the overall convolution that the pattern is termed *awan larat*. As the term suggests, the pattern is compared to moving clouds buffetted by the wind, ever-shifting and difficult to read. Works of this design are among some of the most highly esteemed examples of Malay embroidery. Unfortunately, proficiency in *awan larat* has declined, and such works are rarely undertaken anymore.

In conclusion, gold-thread embroidery is an integral aspect of the Malay decorative arts. Its rich and sumptuous effect is reflected through a technique which demands fine and meticulous crafts-manship. Although it lacks variegated colours, Malay embroidery work remains outstanding in its use of graceful natural motifs and subtle organic styles. The use of glittering gold thread couched work in the finest stitching technique, juxtaposed with dark-coloured base fabrics to delineate the intricate patterns, gives the embroidery a magnificent shimmering appearance. The pieces embellished by embroidery are in themselves unique creations that epitomise the distinctive cultural identity of their creators and embody the rich aesthetic heritage of the Malay community. If nothing else, the craftsmen and women who dedicate themselves to this art have, through their imaginative interpretation, trans-formed the beauty and majesty of their natural surroundings into a worthy art form.

FACING PAGE: A TWO-LAYERED BRIDAL MAT FROM KUALA KANGSAR, PERAK, WORKED IN GOLD THREAD, SPANGLES AND BLUE BEADS OVER RED VELVET AND PINK CHIFFON. THE PATTERN SHOWN HERE COMPRISES ORGANICALLY STYLED BAMBOO SHOOT, FOUR-PETALLED FLOWER, SIX-LEAF CLOVER AND SPIRAL MOTIFS.

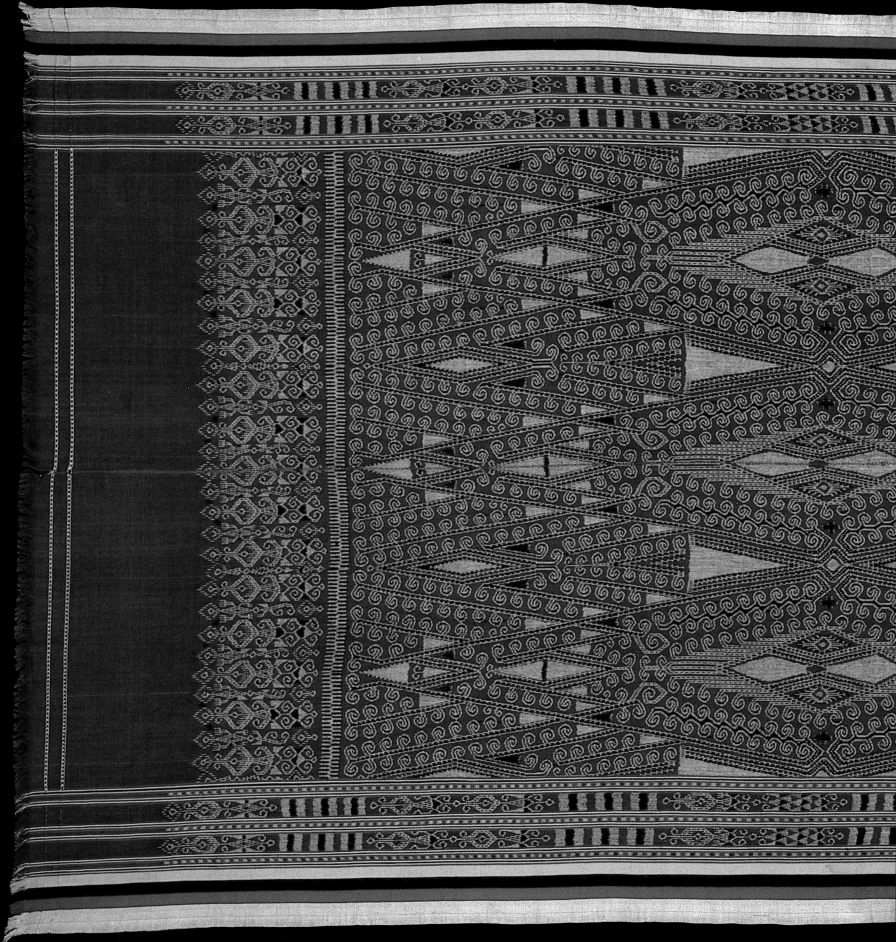

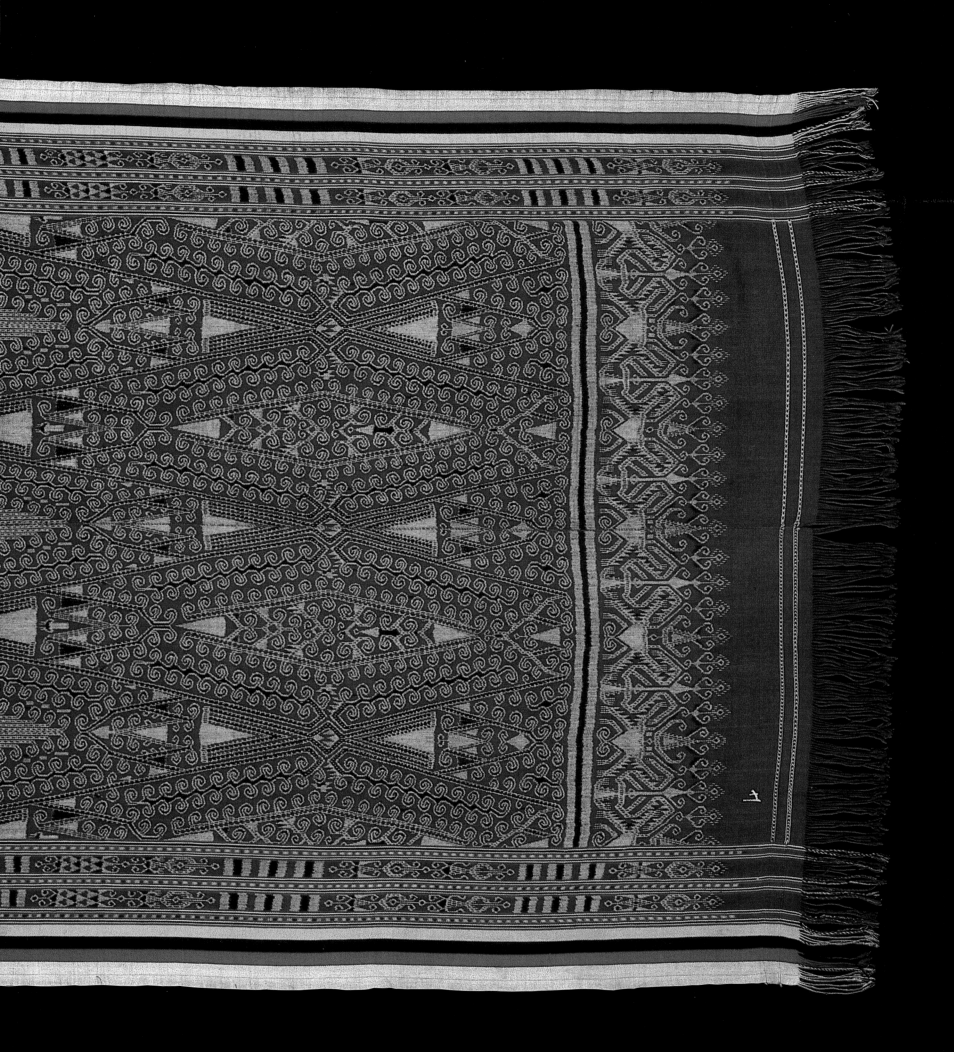

THE PUA KUMBU: SACRED BLANKET OF THE IBAN OF SARAWAK

by Vernon Art Kedit

To the Iban of Sarawak, the *pua kumbu* is not just a blanket. It is a sacred ceremonial and ritual textile. The word *pua* in Iban means 'blanket'; *kumbu* means 'to wrap'. Together, the two words mean a 'grand blanket'. However, the *pua kumbu* is very seldom used as a sleeping blanket. It is reserved for the times when men and women seek an encounter with the spiritual.

Commentators often miss the point that the weaving of an Iban textile, especially the *pua kumbu*, represents a deeply spiritual and socio-religious undertaking. It is a sacred activity that is incumbent upon every Iban woman, so as to establish her womanhood and worth in a society where gender roles are specific, and where spirituality is intrinsically linked to every aspect of daily life. As a weaver, she takes her place in the spiritual regeneration of the traditional values and religious norms of her people.

Iban oral history, mythology and cosmology reverberate with the use of textiles as sacred cloths. Iban *adat* or law, preserved and embodied within Iban oral literature, prescribes the use of textiles as sacred accoutrements at rituals and ceremonies. The earliest mention of the use of textiles as sacred objects appears in Iban creation myths; the first man and woman who were brought to life by the shouts of Raja Entala Keri Raja Petara, the Ancient Creator God, were created under a *pua kumbu*. According to this account, the *pua kumbu* is believed to have already existed at the beginning of time, even before man was created, and its use as a sacred ritual object throughout Iban history preordained.

IBAN TEXTILE CREATION

The ancient Iban wove their daily ceremonial and ritual textiles on the simple back strap tension loom. Rough threads or *ubong* of home-grown cotton called *taya empelai* were the only material available. Towards the end of the nineteenth century, Chinese boat hawkers or *lampu cina* began trading pre-spun cotton threads, both coloured and clear, along the rivers of the 2nd Division in Sarawak. The availability of such threads contributed significantly to the weaving of textiles of finer quality.

The Iban traditionally colour their threads with natural and vegetable dyes obtained from the rainforest. Leaves, barks, root scrappings, vines, seeds, flowers, wood ash, palm salt, nut oil, chalk-lime and fruits of wild and cultivated plants were ingeniously used to extract colours ranging from the lightest beige and pink to the darkest blue, chocolate brown and ash black. The Iban, however, are famed for their unique deep maroon red colour which is obtained from the root scrappings of the *engkudu* tree (*morinda citrifolia spp.*). The work of dyeing textiles takes many days, sometimes months, and is principally the work of women. The method is laborious, and as vegetable dyes never give a consistent result, it is the expertise of the weaver in preparing her concoctions and blending her tones that determines the shades and hues ultimately achieved. Dye recipes are closely guarded family secrets.

The principle weaving technique employed by the Iban is layered warp-ikat or *kebat enggau pampul*. *Ikat* is the resist-dyeing process in which designs are reserved in warp yarns by tying off small bundles of

PRECEDING PAGES: A *PUA KUMBU* WOVEN BY SENDI ANAK KETIT (1892-1974). THE ENTIRE CLOTH COMBINES THEMES OF IBAN CREATION MYTH, ANCIENT GODS, AND THE GREAT IBAN PADI CULT. FACING PAGE: CLOSE-UP OF A *RANYAI BEDUJU* WOVEN BY MENGAN ANAK BUDIN GERASI (1853-1943). A PICTORIAL NARRATIVE OF THE EPIC *GAWAI BURONG* (BIRD FESTIVAL), THIS PARTICULAR PIECE IS RESERVED FOR USE AT ONLY THE MOST SACRED OF CEREMONIES AND RITUALS.

the warp yarns with beeswax-coated fibres of a palm leaf to prevent the dye from penetrating. For each colour, additional tying or partial removal of the bindings is required. After the last dyeing, all bindings are removed and the yarns are ready for weaving (Maxwell 1990: 417).

The Iban are also familiar with other methods of weaving, especially variations on the supplementary weft technique. Textiles, especially ceremonial dress, are also additionally decorated with bells, buttons, beads, cowrie shells, fish scales, coins or amulets. A warrior may sew onto his ceremonial vest the hair of slain enemies as a mark of his exploits. In the old days, vests and loincloths were fashioned from barkcloth extracted from the bark of the *pedalai* tree.

Gold and silver threads are reserved for the finer ceremonial textiles. Rich aristocratic Iban families of the 19th and early 20th centuries, particularly of the Batang Saribas river system, could afford such luxuries and there began the fashion of using such threads as demonstrations of wealth and status. This display of lavish opulence still prevails today.

STATUS AND SPIRITUALITY OF WEAVING

Creating textiles is a discipline governed by specific rules of ancient origin revealed to the ancient Iban by the Iban goddesses of weaving, *Kumang* and *Lulong*. The making of all Iban textiles, in particular the *pua kumbu*, takes on a ritualised form. The Iban believe that every *pua kumbu* contains a spirit which generates a supernatural force, imbuing the cloth with spiritual potency. When a weaver begins work on a *pua kumbu*, she enters a precarious spiritual state where her spirit is in contention with that of the *pua kumbu* she is creating. She must 'capture' the spirit of the *pua kumbu*, which had its 'spiritual birth' in the Iban Hades, *Sebayan*, and must ultimately 'translate' it onto the finished work, where it will have its 'natural birth'. When the weaver has successfully completed her *pua kumbu*, she is deemed to have triumphed over its spirit. With every *pua kumbu* she successfully creates, the weaver's spiritual strength is enhanced.

However, if a weaver transgresses, wilfully or ignorantly, any ritual or technical rule of weaving, she may incur divine displeasure. To contradict the prescribed order and tradition of textile creation is expressly forbidden. The unfortunate weaver is then said to be spiritually vulnerable and may be visited with nightmares, ill-health, madness, or in the extreme, death. The only solution is immediately to abandon work altogether for a period of time and make sacrificial offerings to the goddesses.

The Iban further believe that a weaver with a weak spirit may also be vulnerable to personal tragedy, as a consequence of her spirit being 'consumed' by that of the *pua kumbu* she is weaving. This concept of being spiritually defeated or made impotent is termed *layu*, literally 'to wilt'. The unfinished *pua kumbu* must be completed by another woman of greater experience and spiritual strength. Throughout this entire period of creating textiles, dreams have an important role to play. A weaver would stop all weaving activity if she were to have a nightmare. Conversely, if a weaver has a dream encounter in which one of the goddesses of weaving instructs her in some aspect of the art, she will take this as an endorsement of her growing spiritual maturity. The Iban believe that any dream encounter is spiritual, and all such encounters are acknowledged as dangerous. Thus, to survive such an experience is

AN EARLY 20TH CENTURY *BALI BELUMPONG* FROM THE SARIBAS IBAN. THE STARK IMAGERY OF HEAD TROPHIES, SCREAMING SPIRIT FIGURES AND DECAPITATED CORPSES SPEAKS POWERFULLY OF THE VALUES OF MALE AGGRESSION AND BRAVERY, AS FORMERLY RITUALISED THROUGH THE PRACTICE OF HEADHUNTING. SUCH A CLOTH WAS ALSO UNDERSTOOD TO BE A PERSONAL STATEMENT BY THE WEAVER OF HER SPIRITUAL MATURITY IN WEAVING.

perceived as a mark of spiritual strength. It is also through dreams that mature weavers are sometimes inspired to compose original designs, which are regarded as especially potent as they are the result of powerful encounters with the spiritual. Thus, when an Iban woman undertakes to learn weaving, she is embarking on a road that signals her initiation into the realm of the spiritual, discerning the deeper dimension of *adat* or Iban law and gaining a deeper appreciation of her people's tradition and culture.

Every finished *pua kumbu* bestows upon the weaver spiritual enhancement and improved status within the community. In the old days, the traditional Iban woman regarded the discipline of weaving as an endorsement of her worth. Depending upon the spiritual and technical maturity of her work, it was the principal way by which she obtained and enhanced her status within the community. Thus, the traditional Iban woman viewed her success in life by her status within the female prestige-system.

This prestige-system was a hierachy of ascending degrees of status-rank based on weaving achievements. Each woman was valued according to her merit as a weaver. The highest status-rank was that of the *indu tau nakar tau ngar*, or 'She Who Knows the Secret Measurements and Leads the Ritual of the Dew'. This highest status-rank could really only be achieved by women who were born to it, into families of 'inherited' spiritual strength and the highest social position. Women from these families guarded the rituals of the mordant bath, and the secret methods by which they achieved the elusive rich burgundy colour of their *pua kumbu*. It was not unusual for certain families to have boasted unbroken lines of master weaver-creators. Not only would such a master exhibit unmatched technical skill and spiritual maturity in her weaving, she would also be thoroughly conversant with Iban oral literature and would lead in the chanting of esoteric rites in major ceremonies. Such a 'supreme' woman would often be the recognised authority in matters feminine and supernatural — a position of much honour which every traditional Iban woman aspires to achieve.

THE SPIRITUALITY OF SYMBOLS

The repertoire of images and designs found on Iban textiles is extensive. The flora and fauna of the rainforests of Borneo provide the keen mind with wild animate images, allowing the mature weaver to draw inspiration from both her world view and the Iban pantheon. The heavens and all their inhabitants would find themselves captured onto cloth; their reflections caught and harnessed to sustain power. Different symbols and designs have evolved through the centuries, each one invested with meaning and potency. In the Batang Saribas river system, the depiction of actual deities and personalities are restricted to only the most experienced and spiritually mature weavers of the aristocracy. Families with ancient weaving traditions own motifs that are 'copyrighted' and whose use speak of kinship, ancient power and privileges. Plagiarism is forbidden; the penalty a terrible curse on the offender.

A novice weaver may copy the simple designs of textiles previously woven by her female ancestors and close contemporaries without much danger to her spirit. She has the freedom to compose and express her own interpretation of a classic or famous design, so long as the basic design bears some semblance to the original. On the other hand, the mature weaver may compose a completely original design, motif or symbol, although she risks being perilously exposed to the powerful spirit of the new

design. Spiritual maturity is a necessary prerequisite. The only overriding onus on all weavers, whether novices or master weavers, is that they ensure that the use of symbols and motifs in composing the overall design is conventional, and in keeping with the ancient rules of weaving.

Nevertheless, one must be emphatic in stressing that patterns, motifs and symbols by and in themselves are largely insignificant. Simply alienating and identifying specific motifs for the purpose of attributing special importance to them, without fully grasping the whole compositional design, is as good as not being able to see the forest for the trees. Moreover, such callousness simply offends the very heart of the *raison d'etre* of weaving, which is principally a spiritual undertaking.

Therefore, to appreciate the 'story' of any *pua kumbu* fully, one must fully appreciate the life of its weaver-creator, the times in which it was created, and ultimately possess a comprehensive and near encyclopaedic knowledge of Iban history, pantheon, mythology, lore and law. A *pua kumbu* can thus be perceived as one large canvas upon which its weaver has given expression to her personal understanding of her relationship with the spiritual realm. In short, every design tells a tale, be it a pictorial poem, a legendary narrative, a spiritual offering or even a wild fantasy on a conceptual theme. The weaver becomes not only an artist but also a storyteller, archivist, historian and commentator.

THE RITUAL FUNCTIONS AND USES OF PUA KUMBU

Iban mythology recounts that ancient Iban were taught by a cultural hero called Sera Gunting the use of the *pua kumbu* in receiving head trophies. Sera Gunting especially prescribed that women, where possible, use the great *pua kumbu* called *Lebor Api Mansau Tisi Dilah Kendawang* or 'The Blazing All-Consuming Fire with Edges Coloured like the Tongue of the Krait' (in short, *lebor api*), when ceremonially receiving freshly smoked head trophies from their warrior husbands or suitors on their return from successful war expeditions. The power of the consuming fire harnessed within such a blanket is believed to have been so potent that it would have disarmed any malevolence emanating from the head trophies, which were themselves potent symbols of the Iban fertility cult and male martial aggression. Only the most spiritually powerful master weavers would have braved the challenge to weave the ominous *lebor api*.

Although the *lebor api* is rare, most aristocratic Iban families boast at least one heirloom *lebor api* which would have been used for its intended purpose in the old days of headhunting. The *lebor api* is different from other *pua kumbu* in that it is not made by the *ikat* method but is laboriously woven by the *sungkit* (weft-wrapping) method. Although *lebor api* may come in many different pictorial designs, their one common characteristic is the rich maroon red colour of the *engkudu* dye referred to as *mansau* by the Iban, a representation of the consuming fire.

Besides harnessing supernatural forces and furnishing spiritual protection upon individuals or families, *pua kumbu* also provide a transcendental element in creating a link between the human and spiritual dimension during specific occasions. This is given expression by the concept of sacred ritual space. *Pua kumbu* are used to define sacred ritual space at any number of ceremonies — marriage feasts, funeral and mortuary rituals, padi cultivation rituals, and ritual purification and healing. In all these ceremonies, the *pua kumbu* serve to protect and strengthen those whose souls are undergoing a dangerous transition or journey — such as the recently deceased, the dirge singer who accompanies the departed on part of his journey to the afterlife, the bridal couple embarking on a new journey through life. Indeed, the *pua kumbu* literally accompanies the Iban throughout his entire life, from birth to death and beyond.

By virtue of their potency and value, *pua kumbu* are also used as ritual currency. The Iban *manang* almost always requires an *ikat* skirt called *kain kebat*, or a simple *pua kumbu*, depending on the ritual performed, as payment for his or her services. Iban fines, both ritual and legal, include the use of *pua kumbu* as payment in the case of major offences. And the dowry of a bride is never complete without textiles.

As the possession of *pua kumbu* in traditional society demonstrated wealth, status, prestige and power, it was incumbent upon the women of aristocratic families to create new cloths of the finest quality. *Pua kumbu* and other Iban textiles are passed down through the family, to be used and treasured as heirlooms. In today's world, they have become relics of the past, of the colourful ceremonies and sacred rituals once celebrated by renowned ancestors.

An example of such a ceremony is the esoteric *Gawai Burong*, or Festival of the Bird of the Iban of the Batang Saribas river system. *Pua kumbu* bearing graphic representations of palm-like trees are displayed around a shrine made of a post symbolising the eighth degree of the *Gawai Burong*, which is called *tiang ranyai* (there are altogether nine degrees of the *Gawai Burong*, each degree reflecting the spiritual maturity of the celebrant). The *ranyai* is the great sacred palm that flourishes in *sebayan*, the Iban afterlife; it is a recurring symbol of strength and prestige. A celebrant wishing to sponsor a *Gawai Burong* must be a brave warrior or an aristocratic leader of great prestige, and he may only sponsor the *Gawai Burong* degree by degree, until the cycle of nine is complete.

Likewise, only women of parallel status-rank would dare weave-create *pua kumbu* bearing sacred motifs and designs of the nine degrees of the *Gawai Burong*, especially the sacred design of the *ranyai*. The ninth degree, called *Gerasi Papa* or 'the ravenous giant demon' of the *Gawai Burong*, is rarely ever achieved or celebrated. Its expression onto cloth by great master weavers is very rare indeed.

MODERN TRENDS AND THE DEMYSTIFICATION OF IBAN TEXTILES

The social, political and economic structures of the Iban of Sarawak have seen much change during the latter part of this century. The modern world, with its promise of rapid progress and development, has given rise to an instant materialism culture which exposes traditional Iban practices to rapid socio-cultural changes. Employment opportunities, spending power and education have, in part, alienated many Iban from their traditional pursuits.

The contemporary Iban woman also regards the traditional system of status enhancement through weaving as an archaic and redundant activity. University degrees and corporate firms are now her chief concerns. Even when a woman elects to remain in the traditional longhouse community, weaving is relegated to secondary importance, after cash-cropping or some form of wage employment, though it must be said that in some instances this is due to economic necessity.

In short, *pua kumbu* weaving, with all its attendant ritualism as a sacred feminine activity, has literally gone out of vogue. With the advent of Christian missionary activity, which dispels belief in the old gods, the link with the spiritual is being eroded in many Iban communities. The increasing disintegration of traditional culture and religion has rendered rituals and textiles redundant. Consequently, the necessity for contemporary Iban women to weave sacred ceremonial textiles is no longer there.

In the few places where Iban textiles are still woven and the old tradition practised, ancient motifs and designs have been preserved and sometimes reinterpreted to accommodate and encapsulate modern portrayals of traditional Iban values. The work of master weaver Nicholas Bryan Entarey (one of the very few contemporary Iban male weavers) reflects his concern for the traditional. His intrusion into an otherwise female domain in a society where gender roles are defined has not been ridiculed but welcomed. He has resurrected and highlighted the importance of the traditional values and methods of *pua kumbu* weaving among his contemporaries. Although his designs draw from classical themes, his unique modern interpretation of them expresses and radiates exuberance, boldness and integrity.

Nevertheless, there is an alarming tendency amongst many contemporary weavers to oversimplify designs as well as methods. *Pua kumbu* of handspun cotton dyed with natural vegetable dyes have given way to synthetic cotton yarns and 'modern' colours brewed from cheap instant aniline dyes. This dilution in method is probably due to the constraints of time and an unwillingness to work the laborious and meticulous *kebat* method of old, but it also betrays a disturbing lack of interest demonstrated by contemporary weavers in the esoteric knowledge and rituals of traditional *pua kumbu* creation.

Souvenir-type textiles are produced in bulk at craft centres and adopted villages. These joint-ventures are sponsored by concerned agencies in the hope of preserving traditional handicrafts, sustaining ethnic entrepreneurship and marketing tribal art to a wider audience. The recent innovative production of contemporary quality Iban silk textiles employing traditional methods by Iban weavers of Rumah Atong, Batang Rejang has generated interest within the fashion industry, both locally and abroad. In short, commercial frontiers are being explored for Iban textiles. It is uncertain and questionable whether such ventures will be able to stimulate and sustain the pure, sacred tradition of weaving, as the two methods are in contradiction with each other. The contemporary method is to mass produce ethnic textiles for a large tourist market, where commercial viability is the driving force, while the traditional method is a sacred expression of Iban values demonstrating status and spiritual maturity, with no thought of profit margins.

The future for Iban traditional textile weaving, however, does not look too bleak. It is not unrealistic to envisage that the mass restoration of traditional Iban textile weaving as a sacred spiritual undertaking amongst Iban women can be realised through, and with a renaissance of, Iban culture as a whole. This can be achieved through a true understanding and appreciation of Iban traditional values and lifestyle by the Iban themselves. There is no need for a return to the old religion. However, there is an urgent and dire need for the Iban to live the tradition and values so deeply held by his *aki ini*, his forefathers, lest his rich culture pass him by, swallowed up by the instant and impressive high-tech lifestyle of the 21st century.

FACING PAGE:
THE ENIGMATIC *LEBOR*
API (BLAZING FIRE), ONE
OF THE MOST SACRED OF
IBAN CLOTHS. THIS PIECE
IS WOVEN BY THE WEFT-
WRAPPING METHOD AND
IS MADE UP OF TWO
SELVAGES STITCHED
ONTO A BROAD CENTRAL
PANEL BEARING THE
REPETITIVE MOTIF OF
SQUARE PENDANT
BLOSSOMS WITH HAIR-
LIKE PROJECTIONS (A
CLOSE-UP IS SHOWN ON
THIS PAGE). THE ENTIRE
CLOTH ENDORSES THE
RITUAL OF TAKING
HUMAN HEADS IN
BATTLE, AND WOULD
HAVE BEEN USED BY
THE WOMEN OF THE
LONGHOUSE COMMU-
NITY TO RECEIVE NEW
AND FRESHLY SMOKED
HEAD TROPHIES FROM
THEIR WARRIOR MEN
IN THE OLD DAYS
OF HEADHUNTING.

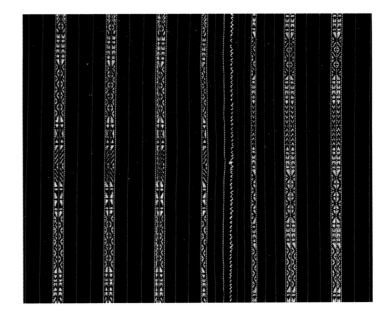

LEFT: A RUNGUS
WEAVER FROM KAMPUNG
TINANGOL SEATED WITH
LEGS STRETCHED OUT
AND WEAVING ON A
BACK STRAP OR
BODY-TENSION LOOM.
THE LARGE SWORD-LIKE
WOODEN IMPLEMENT IS
A BEATER USED TO BEAT
THE WEFT THREADS
TO PACK THEM IN.
BELOW: A CLOSE-UP OF A
KNEE-LENGTH SKIRT OR
TAPI, WORN BY THE
RUNGUS OF SABAH.

METALS

The most abundant metal found in Malaysia is tin, the richest deposits being in the Kinta valley of Perak and the Klang Valley in Selangor. Base metals like copper, lead and zinc have been discovered in Ulu Sokor, Kelantan and Tasik Cini and the Mengapur area in Pahang.

Currently, the largest copper mine in Malaysia is situated in Ranau, Sabah. Small veins of gold have been found along the central axial belt from Kelantan through to Pahang, Negri Sembilan and Johor, and gold is presently mined at the Bau District in Sarawak. Iron ore is mined on a very small scale in Pahang, Kedah, Perak and Johor, while the Sarawak river delta in East Malaysia exported iron in the 10th to 14th centuries. Metal working has been an established industry in all parts of Malaysia for several centuries, in forms ranging from heavy weaponry to the most delicate jewellery. In all areas of manufacture local craftsmen, although using simple tools, have achieved a high standard of workmanship.

BRASS

The origins of brass, which is an alloy of copper and zinc, can be traced to the earlier art of casting bronze, a mixture of copper and tin. Bronze working in Southeast Asia dates back to about 3,000 BC, from the evidence of archaeological finds in Ban Chiang and Non Nok Tha in northern Thailand. The methods employed by these ancient craftsmen eventually spread across the Malay Archipelago.

The art of casting brass was most likely introduced into Malaya from Thailand about three hundred years ago, and was centred in and around Kuala Terengganu. Traditionally, cottage industries like gold- and silversmithies thrived under the patronage of the Malay royal households who required domestic and ceremonial objects made from these precious metals. The brass industry, on the other hand, owes its existence more to ordinary villagers who, being unable to afford precious metals, used objects made from brass. These included kettles, large serving trays, bowls, large cooking pots with lids and heavy buckets for raising well water.

As time progressed, the art of brass casting evolved into a craft industry producing smaller domestic pieces of traditional design for decorative use and for the domestic religious ceremonies of the ordinary Malay household. These included such items as candlesticks and candelabras, flower vases, ashtrays, incense burners, dispensers for scented water and *sireh* sets which are made from white brass. Brass was also used to make moulds for casting tin currency.

The *sireh* set — composed of various small containers which hold the ingredients for the betel chew — was once the pivot around which Malay social life turned. In a Malay house, the *sireh* set was placed before visitors whenever they called, and they would then be joined by the host in the informal ritual involved in preparing the chew. *Sireh* sets and items such as incense burners and perfume sprinklers were used in the ceremonies performed during Malay betrothals, weddings and funerals. It was therefore uncommon to find a Malay household without these brassware items.

One of the most celebrated pieces made by Terengganu craftsmen is the incense burner which is now part of the Terengganu Museum collection. It was designed and made by two local artisans, Mat bin Omar and Abdullah bin Haji Ali, around 1940. It was made in four separate parts: the cover, charcoal

PRECEDING PAGES:
A MALAY BRASS GONG
FROM SARAWAK.
FACING PAGE: A
DONGSON BRONZE BELL
IN MUZIUM NEGARA,
ONE OF THE FINEST EVER
FOUND IN MALAYSIA.
THIS PAGE: A SCULP-
TURED BRONZE FIGURE
OF A BRAHMIN SAGE.

container, the main body and the base. It measures 119 cm in height and 72.5 cm across and was originally a gift from Sultan Sulaiman Badrul Alam Shah of Terengganu (1920-1942) to Masjid Abidin.

Early bronze cannons can also be attributed to Terengganu craftsmen. The manufacture of such cannons later flourished in Brunei as a result of Terengganu brass-smiths, who went over to start foundries. It was in Brunei that the Malays began to develop an artistic flair for decorating their cannons, using intricate designs based on local motifs, dragons and other beautiful patterns along the muzzles. From Brunei their work was imported into the neighbouring districts of Borneo. Much later the Iban, and to some extent other ethnic groups, began to learn casting methods and created their own styles — cannons with dragons, crocodiles and many other similar designs — for their own purposes.

The Maloh, another indigenous Sarawak group, were well known for their brass-making techniques and habitually travelled along Borneo's rivers offering their services. Among the many items they made were heavy brass earrings traditionally worn by the Iban, Kayan and Kenyah groups. Such earrings, which extend the earlobes of the wearer, were usually cast in sand moulds. Among many Borneo peoples, bronze and brass gongs and cannons were highly prized as family heirlooms and were often presented during betrothals as bridal gifts. Among the Melanau of Sarawak it was once customary to bury brass objects, together with beads and ceramic objects, as grave goods.

The difference between brassware from Sarawak and Terengganu is readily apparent. Sarawak brass objects are usually decorated with figures of real or imaginary animals like the dragon, similar to the brassware attributed to neighbouring Brunei. By contrast, Islam profoundly influences art of the Peninsula, where geometric, floral and calligraphic decorations predominate. Alternatively, the craftsman left his work completely devoid of decoration, as can be seen in the smooth shiny brasses of Terengganu.

TYPES OF BRASSWARE

There are two types of brassware made in Malaysia today, yellow brass for more utilitarian pieces and white brass — with a luxurious mirrored finish — for more decorative items. Both types of brass are mainly cast in the *ciré perdu* or lost wax method. Originally, beeswax obtained from the wild was used for this purpose but in more recent times wax has been purchased from commercial suppliers in Singapore.

Before the craftsman begins casting an item he needs to make a model of the item or a section of it to serve as a master pattern. This is either shaped from a lump of clay or carved out of wood. The model is then immersed several times in hot wax, which is allowed to cool between each application, until a covering of the desired thickness has been built up. In order to accelerate the hardening process the model is dipped into cold water after each coating of wax. When the wax formation is thick enough, the model is removed from the wax shell. The shell is then hand-turned to the required shape or thickness on a simple foot-operated string lathe.

The wax shell is then covered with three different layers of local clay. The first layer is unadulterated clay, the second a composition of clay and fine beach sand, and the third, clay mixed with rice husks. The moulds are dried in the open for several days between each application. Each of the

A ROSE-WATER SPRINKLER, A TERENGGANU BRASS OBJECT WHICH IS A COMMON SIGHT IN ANY MALAY HOME.

three layers of clay is applied for a specific purpose. The initial layer is best suited for retaining a clear impression from the wax; the second offsets shrinkage in the final layer when it is fired; and the mixture of clay and rice husks prevents cracking when the clay dries out.

When the moulds have dried they are heated for about an hour in a charcoal-fired pit furnace, together with the crucible containing the molten metal. The furnace, some 60 cm deep and measuring from a half-metre to a metre in diameter, is normally made of ordinary bricks and is worked by manually operated traditional bellows or an electric motor blower. The heat of the furnace causes the wax to melt and drain away. Molten metal is then poured from a crucible into the hollow moulds via the hole through which the wax escaped. Any leaks in the clay are immediately sealed with fresh wet clay. After the moulds have cooled and the baked clay has been broken off, the cast brass is examined for any flaws, which are then removed and filled with tin or lead solder. In order to disguise the repair work, a mixture of gold and aluminium crystals in varnish is rubbed into the spot. Articles which have been cast in separate pieces are assembled by soldering. The items are then polished manually on a simple string lathe. The fine shine on white brass is achieved through the use of emery paper.

The composition of local brassware is not uniform and varies according to family formulae, from between one to four parts of brass to one of nickel and one quarter of zinc. Yellow brass is composed of one part zinc to every eight parts of scrap brass. The better quality white brass contains more zinc and a quantity of nickel. In the last two centuries, the supply of metal to craftsmen has been erratic. Formerly, Chinese traders who sailed along the coast of Malaya imported the metal or sold strings of old Chinese 'cash' coins for the purpose. In more recent times the metals used were obtained from Singapore, but in times of scarcity it was derived from spent brass cartridges and shell cases, ship piping and scrap brass.

Most of the items produced today are bought by the local population and tourists. Although the demand for brassware still exists, supply cannot meet demand. This is due to several factors, one of which is the irregular supply of raw materials. The method of manufacture, too, is laborious and outmoded, but craftsmen are reluctant to introduce new processes and techniques. This has created an apathy among the younger generation, who see no future in the business. Unless something can be done to inject new life into the industry, the current decline will lead to its eventual demise.

The most established craftsman in the traditional brass industry is Wan Ismail bin Osman, whose family has been in the same business for five generations. His operation in Terengganu, which is a typical example of such localised and small-scale businesses, is centred around the family home under which his workshop is situated. The forge is located a safe distance away in a corner of the compound. Most of his workers are family members or neighbours, many of whom help out sporadically in between their own domestic chores. His most recent commission, ordered by the Ministry of Culture, was for several sets of small brass gongs for the *caklempong*, a percussion instrument which forms part of the orchestra used by local *gamelan* groups. The manufacture of these instruments died out many years ago, but with the recent revival of traditional Malay music, there is a new demand for them. With the commission from the Ministry of Culture, an age-old tradition of patronage has been re-established.

FACING PAGE: A TYPICAL
MALAY *GAMELAN*
ORCHESTRA OF PAHANG
DURING THE LATE 1800'S.
THE *GAMELAN* — WHICH
IS COMPOSED OF BRASS
GONGS OF VARIOUS
SIZES, XYLOPHONES, TWO
BARREL-DRUMS AND A
VIOLIN — PLAYS A
PROMINENT PART IN THE
ACCOMPANIMENT OF THE
MALAY DANCE TO
WELCOME THE SULTAN
ON CEREMONIAL
OCCASIONS.

THIS PAGE: THIS FORM
OF SOLID TIN CURRENCY,
MADE IN THE SHAPE OF
VARIOUS ANIMALS
INCLUDING THE
CROCODILE, WAS FIRST
USED IN THE MALAY
STATES OF PERAK,
SELANGOR AND NEGRI
SEMBILAN DURING THE
15TH CENTURY. IT WAS
INITIALLY USED AS GIFTS
TO ROYALTY AND FOR
MAGICAL RITES
ASSOCIATED WITH THE
TIN MINING COMMUNITY.
LATER IT EVOLVED AS A
FORM OF CURRENCY IN
THE MALAY STATES.

FACING PAGE, TOP:
A CRAFTSMAN IS SEEN
APPLYING THE LAST
LAYER OF FINE CLAY
ON THE WAX MODEL
OF A CAULDRON.
FACING PAGE, BOTTOM:
THE WAX MODELLED
CAULDRONS WHICH
HAVE BEEN LAYERED
WITH CLAY ARE PLACED
IN A CHARCOAL-FIRED PIT
FURNACE TO MELT AND
DRAIN AWAY THE WAX.
THIS PAGE: RED HOT
MOLTEN BRASS IS POURED
INTO A MOULD TO
PRODUCE AN OBJECT
WHICH HAS ALREADY
BEEN MODELLED FROM
WAX. THIS TRADITIONAL
METHOD, WHICH IS
UNIVERSALLY PRACTISED,
IS KNOWN AS THE *CIRÉ
PERDU* PROCESS.

THIS PAGE:
THE INTERIOR OF
ISTANA TELE IN KUALA
TERENGGANU, SHOWING
THE POSITION OF
CEREMONIAL GIFTS
PLACED IN FRONT OF A
ROYAL DIAS. IN THIS
SCENE, THERE ARE FOUR
MEDIUM AND ONE LARGE
BRASS PEDESTAL TRAYS,
EACH CONTAINING A
MOUND OF YELLOW
GLUTINOUS RICE. RISING
FROM EACH IS A
MINIATURE TREE WITH
HARD-BOILED EGGS
WRAPPED IN GOLD FOIL
HANGING FROM EACH
BRANCH. A BRASS
SPITTOON SITS BY EACH
PILLAR IN THE
FOREGROUND.
FACING PAGE: BRASS
KETTLES FROM SARAWAK
(TOP) AND TERENGGANU
(BOTTOM). THE ROUNDED
BODY OF THE KETTLE, ITS
SPOUT, HANDLE AND
DECORATIVE ADDITIONS
WERE ALL CAST
SEPARATELY BY THE
CIRÉ PERDU PROCESS
AND SUBSEQUENTLY
WELDED TOGETHER.

IRON

For the past several hundred years, in Peninsula Malaysia and the states of Sabah and Sarawak in Borneo, iron has been used predominantly for the manufacture of blades, for weaponry as well as for domestic use. For at least seven hundred years, Malay blacksmiths have forged a variety of weapons of war, including cannons, slashing weapons, kris and short daggers of various shapes and sizes. In Borneo, too, metalsmiths have been making fine weapons comparable to those of European manufacture, for example, the Kenyah and Kayan swords from Sarawak. Some of the very old *parang* made by the Iban and the orang ulu in Sarawak also demonstrate a high quality of workmanship.

In the past, since iron ore was not mined in commercial quantities locally, blacksmiths bartered for slabs or strips of the metal from foreign traders. Twentieth century smiths, however, found that scrap iron such as old car springs made an ideal substitute from which to shape a strong and reliable blade. In the early days a homemade domestic forge existed in most rural villages, where the ironsmiths worked in their spare time when they were not occupied in the padi fields or with fishing.

In order to fan the fire in the forge, blacksmiths used a crude form of homemade bellows often operated by children or a village elder. Air is forced down two hollow logs or large bamboo tubes by means of a piston tightly bound with strong cloth or layers of feathers. The bellows worked along lines similar to a pair of bicycle pumps working in tandem to produce a continuous stream of air. On the downward stroke, the piston rods force the air occupying the logs down and out through clay tubes into the charcoal fire, while the upward stroke sucks in a fresh supply of air with each intake. Another type of bellows once in use took the form of a wooden rectangular box which was placed alongside the fire and separated from it by a clay wall. It worked on a similar principle whereby a square piston was pushed in and out to create a gush of air into the fire. Unlike modern blacksmiths who use conventional iron anvils and who have an array of up-to-date tools at their disposal, the first ironsmith's anvil was simply a large slab of solid rock, while his hammer was just a stone lashed onto a wooden flexible handle.

A fine example of a blade from a bygone era is the headhunter's *parang ilang* from Sarawak. These were forged in the usual manner: by repeatedly heating and folding the red hot slab or rod and hammering it into the shape of a blade. When the desired shape had been achieved, the blade was hardened by plunging it into water. The curly decoration on the back of the blade was accomplished by chiseling notches into the hot metal, then forging the points longer and bending them with pincers. As an added embellishment a pattern was inlaid in silver or brass. The most exacting part of the process was grinding and polishing the edge with sandstone until it was razor sharp. Finally, using a composition of various materials like ivory, bone, horn and wood, a decorative hilt was carved and affixed to the blade, which was then encased in a scabbard made from the same elements. Today, the *parang ilang* is made only for the tourist market and is highly prized as an authentic souvenir.

The use of metals differs from one blade to another. A good example is the kris blade, which is normally composed of between two to seven thin layers of different types of iron. Occasionally there might be as many as twenty-one different layers. The blade which is believed to have belonged to the

legendary 15th century hero Hang Tuah, in the court of the Melaka Sultanate, was said to have many more different layers of metal. The Malay craftsmen of Melaka established a reputation for producing fine metalwork, in a tradition which can be traced back to the Majapahit Empire of Java in the 13th century. When the empire collapsed two centuries later, many craftsmen migrated to other parts of the Malay Archipelago and later to the Malay Peninsula. Melaka then took the lead in producing the kris. During the Melaka period, the kris developed into something more than a lethal weapon: it became a prestigious status symbol of the upper hierarchy, an item of adornment and a token of spiritual strength.

The kris

Although in modern times the kris is no longer associated with the rich and powerful, to some it still remains an object of mystery, believed to possess spiritual power, and to have the ability to protect the owner from physical harm and misfortune. Traditionally, a kris of this description was revered and treated according to certain rites and rituals in order to appease the spiritual element which, it was believed, inhabited the weapon. Ill-treatment or neglect might cause the guardian spirit to depart for its home in the spiritual world, leaving the kris powerless.

Although some kris blades are made solely from iron, most are alloyed with another metal, usually nickel, which is placed along either side of the iron and pounded repeatedly to produce a damasked effect. The typical wavy edge of the kris blade is achieved by repeatedly reheating the metal and hammering the edges of the blade against the side of the anvil. Provided the blacksmith is well-equipped, it takes him no longer than a day to make a good blade.

The superiority of the kris, particularly one believed to possess supernatural powers, is judged according to the *pamur* or damascening of the blade, and the quality of the alloys used. Importantly, the kris must be compatible with its owner. The length of the blade should correspond to the distance between the nipples of its owner, otherwise misfortune might befall him. A well-balanced mature blade is considered more potent. Many kris have become family heirlooms, and are thought to be more powerful by virtue of their association with previous generations.

The correct way to begin measuring a kris is to press both thumbs against the flat surface at the base of the blade and move along, placing one thumb after the other along the blade, ending at the tip. Harmony between a kris and its owner would be judged by the number of thumb counts taken. The ideal number is predetermined by a medium who has been in contact with the spirit of the kris.

A kris would not be complete without a hilt and sheath, requiring the skill of different craftsmen, including the wood carver and the silversmith. Sometimes ivory or horn are used to make the hilt and scabbard, while the other parts are covered with silver over wood. Today, the most magnificent hilts and sheaths may be seen in the regalia of Malay royalty. Royal weapons are often embellished with gold and silver beautifully engraved with traditional motifs. In his regalia, the Sultan of Perak has the kris believed to be the *Taming Sari*, the famous kris Hang Tuah brought back to Melaka. The kris is now beautifully embedded with gemstones on the hilt and sheath.

One look around a souvenir shop will tell you that the kris is still popular, although now simply as an item of decoration. Nevertheless, the persistence of the kris form is a reminder of the glories of the olden days, when Malay warriors battled enemies using these unique yet lethal weapons.

Other weapons

Besides the kris, many other types of thrusting and cutting weapons are found in the Peninsula and in the states of Sarawak and Sabah. Some of these are obviously foreign introductions of Arabic or Indian design, while others appear to be of native origin or introduced from neighbouring states like Sulu, Celebes, Java and Sumatra. All these weapons use iron alloy for the blade.

Another important iron weapon is the *ekor lotong*, a Malay cannon whose name translates into 'monkey's tail' in Malay. This cannon was made using the same *ciré perdu* or lost wax process that was used for similar brass weapons. Cannon balls were also made from iron. Examples of some of these cannons still remain in the collections of various museums throughout the country.

The most skillful ironsmiths, who trace their descent from a long line of craftsmen, live in Terengganu and Kelantan on the East Coast of Peninsular Malaysia. One ironsmith who still practises the craft is Abu Bakar, who lives in Pasir Panjang on the fringe of Kuala Terengganu. From the day he left school at the age of twelve, he became apprenticed to his grandfather's workshop. By age twenty-one he was already an established ironsmith in his own right. His workshop, which is situated behind his home, is a simple structure made from a few sheets of corrugated iron roofing.

Although he is well-equipped with an array of modern tools, Bakar still uses the traditional bellows, primarily for sentimental reasons, as they belonged to his late grandfather. His workshop is very small, with just enough space for him to move from right to left and arrange his work methodically so that he does not waste time. The heating, beating, shaping and polishing of the blades are all carried out in this confined, yet impeccably organised space. The kris is Bakar's favourite weapon and although the blades that he makes today are ornamental, they are also fine examples of his unique skill and a reminder of the bygone age of the Golden Chersonese. In order to perpetuate his craft, Abu Bakar is now training his son to follow in his footsteps.

During one of my recent field trips, he was happy to learn that his products are accepted by most of the contemporary weapon collectors. This has encouraged him to reproduce other types of traditional weapons. He now prefers to concentrate mainly on producing short daggers, simply because such weapons are fashioned easily and can be sold readily in the open market at reasonable prices. In order to keep his craft going, he also accepts special commissions. These may range from a kris intended for a bridegroom of a noble family, to wear when he sits in state during the marriage ceremony, to a kris meant to be presented to a foreign visitor as a gift from royalty or from a minister of state. Abu Bakar finds such commissions challenging, as they provide him with the stimulus to further perfect his skills. Although listed as among the best makers of traditional Malay weapons today, Abu Bakar clearly has no intention of resting on his laurels.

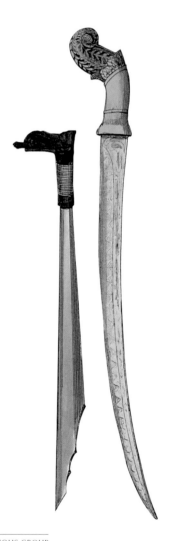

AN INDIGENOUS GROUP
FROM SARAWAK CIRCA
1910 (RIGHT) WORKING
IRON INTO SHAPE TO
FORM WEAPONS (ABOVE).
THEY ARE USING TWIN
WOODEN BELLOWS TO
SUPPLY A CONTINUOUS
FLOW OF AIR FOR
THE FIRE TO SOFTEN
THE METAL.

182   The Crafts of Malaysia

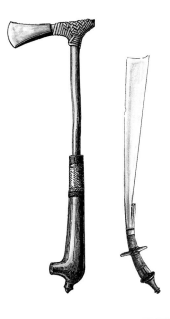

BLACKSMITHS FROM
THE PENINSULA (FACING
PAGE) AND SARAWAK
(THIS PAGE) FASHION
HOT METAL INTO
BLADES. TOOLS LIKE
THE *ADZE* AND *PARANG*
(ABOVE) FROM EAST
MALAYSIA ARE MADE
IN THIS WAY.

GOLD

Owing to the richness of its gold deposits, Peninsular Malaysia was known as the 'Golden Peninsula' and the land of the 'Golden Chersonese' by traders in the global network of the ancient world. Gold flakes of superior quality were mined in Terengganu, and in Gunung Ledang in Johor and Gemencheh in Negeri Sembilan as early as 2,000 years ago.

During the early period of the Melaka Sultanate (1400-1522), payment for goods, particularly tin and spices, was mainly in the form of gold dust which was also brought in from Sumatra, India, Goa, the Middle East and China. Gold coins were not introduced into the Peninsula until the 16th century, when Kelantan issued a coinage bearing the *kijang* or barking deer and floral motifs. Johor and Kedah followed suit with gold coinages of their own a little later. It was these coins that were used by Kelantan and Kedah to make the sheets of gold from which the *bunga mas*, a small golden tree, was fashioned. The *bunga mas*, which stood about one and a half metres tall, was made by the states of Kedah and Kelantan and presented to the King of Siam as an annual tribute. Of the few remaining *bunga mas*, two (one in gold and the other in silver), both of which were made in Kedah, are in the Royal Palace in Bangkok while one other, believed to be of Kelantanese origin, is in the National Museum, Bangkok. A miniature version in gold is in the palace of the Sultan of Kelantan.

The development of the craft of fashioning gold ornaments during that period owed much to the patronage of Malay royalty in the capitals of Kota Bharu, Kuala Terengganu, Kuala Kangsar and Pekan. Goldsmiths who enjoyed privileged positions in the courts often lived with their families near the royal palaces. Gold jewellery and ornaments, exquisitely made and often set with precious stones, reached their peak in popularity during the 17th and 18th centuries.

Pure gold is soft and malleable, so ornaments made from pure gold are easily damaged. Most court jewellery therefore was made from gold which had been mixed with an alloy in order to strengthen it. The goldsmith usually melted his gold in a very small crucible over a charcoal fire which was maintained at a constant temperature by a pair of homemade bellows. Most of the articles were wrought by hand, using simple implements modified to suit the individual goldsmith's taste and style. A conical shaped mallet or small hammer made of buffalo horn — with a layer of soft alloy on the face — is the best type of tool for forming circles, accomplished by bending the metal on its point and beating it with a hammer. Probably the most prized of all the goldsmith's possessions were his handmade punches, which became his signature and the means by which other craftsmen were able to identify his work.

Other important implements included various chisels, tweezers, files, pliers and needle-sharp engraving tools known as scribes. In order to make gold wire, drawplates were used. These were thick flat sheets of metal with graduated holes through which the wire was pulled using a steel mandrel rod.

Though having a number of techniques at their command, traditional Malay goldsmiths were particularly adept at repoussé work and granulation. Repoussé — the art of embossing a pattern in relief onto a thin sheet of gold — was widely used to decorate a variety of ornaments. Granulation, on the other hand, is a laborious and time-consuming method of applying tiny grains of molten gold to the surface of an ornament. Granules are added to provide decoration as well as to help secure individual pieces of gold in place, particularly when an ornament has been composed of several segments, each embossed separately, cut out and soldered together. In Malay work, the granules vary in size, the largest measuring approximately 1.5 mm in diameter. In many cases, before the decoration is applied, the surface of each granule is hammered with a fine flat-tipped punch to produce a faceted effect designed to give added lustre. Goldsmiths also produced small flat discs of various sizes that were applied in the same fashion. The granules and discs, together with gold wires of various thicknesses, were commonly used together to produce beautiful arabesque patterns best illustrated in the necklace or *dokoh*.

Tinting the gold red or orange is another technique which characterises Malay work. Since gold is impervious to most corrosives and never changes colour naturally, a complicated method was devised to produce this effect. The object is first immersed for one or two days in a clay pot containing a mixture of rain, salt and alum. It is then removed and cleaned before being placed in hot embers for about five minutes. During the second stage of the process the gold object is once again immersed in a clay pot containing another mixture of rain, a teaspoon of sulphur and a slice or two of a dried acidic fruit (*Garcinia atnoviridis*) used in flavouring curries. The mixture is boiled for ten minutes and the gold then taken out, cleaned and heated once again over hot embers until it changes colour.

Gold jewellery and ornaments were usually worn by the Malay aristocracy during official ceremonial functions. An important item in the full ceremonial dress of Malay rulers was the *pending* or belt buckle, many of which were enriched with precious gems. Other fine examples of the goldsmith's work are the pendants (*dokoh*) that were inspired by the shape of the *sukun* or breadfruit leaf. Many of these antique gold ornaments were covered with tiny granules of gold known as *telur ikan* or fish eggs, which were carefully polished to catch the light and highlight the piece. Each one took a long time to complete and it is evident that great patience and skill went into producing them.

One of the most unique items produced in this region at that time was the modesty disc or *caping*, a heart-shaped disc designed to cover the genitals of children. At one time these were especially popular in the north and east of Peninsular Malaysia, as well as Sabah and Sarawak. *Caping* were made from a variety of materials, including gold and coconut shell.

Many of the ornamentation styles devised by Malay goldsmiths for their patrons were adopted by other communities like the Chinese, Indians and Portuguese, who migrated to the Peninsula over the centuries. One of these was the habit of wearing the *kerosang*, a set of three identical or matching brooches used to secure an outfit consisting of a blouse worn with a *sarung*. These brooches were often heavily engraved with different designs according to the wearer's taste. Malay women preferred those based on a variation of the breadfruit leaf design, whereas Peranakan women normally chose designs which depicted animal forms or good omens. The Peranakan *kerosang serong* can be easily recognised by its distinctive shape, and was often mounted with rough-cut precious or semi-precious stones.

Most of the wealthy Malay, Portuguese, Indian and Peranakan women secured their hair in a bun with gold or silver hairpins known as *cucuk sanggul*, the longest of these measuring 15 cm. Only one or

two would normally be used, but on festive occasions the pins were worn in graduated sets of three, five or seven. A bride's formal wedding attire also included an elaborate headdress, the crown of which comprised a number of flexible pieces designed to quiver as the bride moved her head. Bracelets and anklets, customarily worn in pairs, were made from thin embossed sheets of gold and were hollow inside. The Malays preferred these ornaments to be decorated with foliated or geometric patterns, whereas Peranakan women showed a preference for the sugar cane or bamboo design.

The custom of chewing tobacco was introduced into this country centuries ago and became firmly established among the Malay, Chinese and Indian communities. Boxes for carrying tobacco were an important part of the Malay regalia, particularly among the royalty and male members of the household, who wore portable tobacco boxes suspended from a chain around their waists. Another popular habit among all the communities was the chewing of *sireh* leaves, a practice which is centuries old. Betel leaf boxes fashioned from gold and inlaid with gems can be found as part of a sultan's regalia.

The beginning of the last century brought about the decline of local goldsmiths. This was partly the result of gold jewellery being imported into the country. Today, only a few Malay master craftsmen remain as they struggle to maintain their skills. Today's gold is fashionable but not of the artistic quality of the past. Although some of the modern craftsmen are no doubt capable of producing replicas of some of the traditional designs from the past, their former beauty can never be entirely recreated.

SILVER

Although silver objects of religious significance have been found in Peninsular Malaysia and Borneo dating back to the Hindu Buddhist eras of the first millennium, silver, unlike gold, is not indigenous to Malaysia. As a result, silversmithing only evolved many centuries later, as an offshoot of an established gold working tradition. Raw materials in the form of silver bars, ingots or coins were imported into the country through foreign traders.

During the 1400's, when the Melaka Sultanate was at its zenith, silver, together with gold, became a symbol of the wealth and power of the Malay aristocracy under whose patronage Malay craftsmen flourished. Among all the known methods of decoration used by Malay gold- and silversmiths, repoussé was the most popular. Embossed patterns were often reminiscent of old Malay wood carvings, based mainly on floral motifs in strict adherence to the teachings of Islam, which prohibited the use of zoomorphic decorations. Among items which have survived to this day are silver bowls, boxes, portable tobacco containers, *sireh* sets, bolster ends and items of personal jewellery like belt buckles.

Malay silversmiths also learned the art of making the enamelled silver known as nielloware from their Thai neighbours in Patani, where it first became established some time during the twelfth century. In order to highlight the lustrous quality of the silver-embossed motifs, a black enamel, composed of metal sulphides, is applied to the recessed parts of the silver's surface. The item is then fired to fuse the enamel before being ground to a smooth finish. Niello was most commonly used on bowls, kettles, betel boxes and belt buckles.

During the 1930's, the shortage of silver and the importation of cheap commercial products brought about the decline of the silver industry. It was then that a group of European planters imported silver through the banks and privately commissioned Malay silversmiths to produce European style tableware as a way of reviving the craft. Examples of these pieces, once owned by Datuk Blaney, are now in the collection of the National Museum in Kuala Lumpur.

Today, the silver industry has been reduced to a few families in the states of Kelantan and Terengganu. Those who operate in Kuala Lumpur, like the Yaacob family who run Tuan Haji Yaacob & Sons Sdn Bhd, have migrated from these East Coast states to establish businesses in the city. Another such company run by Tuan Haji Bakri, called Perniagaan TABA, specialises in modern made-to-order objects such as gifts and medals ordered by the states, and presentation plaques to mark special occasions. In most cases a silversmith will accept a challenge to produce any form of article or object, from the simple to the most intricate.

Among contemporary Malay silversmiths, Kamaruddin Che Mat, who now works in the comfort of the Malaysian Handicraft Training Centre in Kelantan, is recognised among his colleagues for his exceptional skills and experience. He began working with silver at a very young age and is acknowledged as a talented designer. For the past couple of centuries, the methods and techniques of manufacturing Malay silver have remained basically the same. Kamaruddin still uses a common standard-size leather bellows which he operates with his right foot, and a small blowtorch to melt the metal. Since he only works on small items, he has not ventured into using complicated appliances. If the need arises, he normally borrows any additional equipment he might need from friends.

In accordance with traditional methods, once the metal has melted Kamaruddin pours it into a wooden mould which has been coated with domestic coconut oil. When the silver sheet has solidified he removes it with special pincers so as not to damage the surface and quickly plunges it into cold water to harden it. Once this has been done, the next step is to hammer and roll the sheet into a thin lamina so that it is easily bent into shape. Before an article is finished the silver sheet goes through several stages. Kamaruddin usually prepares a hot mixture of molten resin, wax and a little powdered clay which is poured onto the reverse side of the article. When this has set it provides a protective coating for the metal while the silversmith works on the engraving process. Kamaruddin uses two methods to prepare the surface for engraving: he either draws a pattern directly onto the surface with the sharp edge of his chisel, or he draws the pattern on tracing paper and glues it on the convex surface of the silver. In most cases, Kamaruddin uses only traditional motifs of petals, foliage and arabesque coiling vines.

Most of Kamaruddin's engraving tools are modern, while some are those he has made himself along the lines of tools used by Malay wood carvers. Other implements include a variety of small chisels, punches, hammers with selected heads, files, a goldsmith's saw, scissors, pliers and tweezers. With all these tools, he forms curves, circles, lines, dashes, rosettes and tiny stars.

No two objects of the same type and style are ever the same, for Kamaruddin always varies the patterns a little, thereby creating unique works of art. Once the engraving and punchwork have been

FACING PAGE:
AN IBAN MAIDEN
IN CEREMONIAL ATTIRE
CONSISTING OF A
BEAUTIFULLY DESIGNED
TRADITIONAL CORSET
DECORATED WITH COINS.
SHE ALSO HAS ON
ARMLETS, A NECKLACE
AND A HEADDRESS
OF SILVER.

completed, he then melts the resinous base, cleans any flaws and polishes the article to a shine with worn out emery paper before applying a high grade polish. Kamaruddin also recommends the *buah sabun*, juice of the *Sapindas ranak* fruit, to add shine to the silver object.

Among the Chinese communities in Malaysia, silverware was most highly regarded by the Peranakan or Straits Chinese. When the Chinese first came to Melaka in the 1400's, they found brides among the Malay community and settled down. Over the centuries a unique blend of both cultures emerged which was reflected in their dress, language, customs and traditions. Although the Peranakan used silver for much the same purposes as the Malays, Chinese silversmiths developed a distinctive style of their own which was readily distinguishable from the work of their Malay counterparts. Unfortunately, the old traditions have died out and there is no one among the Peranakan community today who can produce silverware on a par with the work of his ancestors.

In Sarawak, people also possess large collections of silver ornaments, most of which form an important part of their ceremonial attire. Headdresses, chains of necklaces, brooches, bangles, bracelets, rings, buttons, pendants and pins for the hair or clasps for securing blouses have, for the past few hundred years anyway, been fashioned from imported silver. The main forms bear a striking resemblance to those worn in Peninsular Malaysia.

The best known silversmiths in Sarawak were the Maloh. For many generations they maintained a high standard of workmanship using traditional styles and methods. Typical examples of Maloh-made silver apparel were the beautiful girdles consisting of numerous lengths of narrow rattan pieces covered in silver rings and joined together. Similar methods were employed to make elaborate silver belts. It is interesting to note that silver belts and buckles were usually not worn about the waist but across the chest and shoulders. Silver ornaments and jewellery were particularly worn by maidens on festive occasions. In most cases, Maloh ornaments were embossed or incised with floral motifs following a set design.

By the 20th century, the Iban preferred to wear belts comprising traded silver coins and crown pieces, as well as smaller denominations of coins issued between the reigns of Queen Victoria to Elizabeth II. Similar belts are also favoured by the Kadazan of Sabah when they wore their traditional costumes for official functions or at the weddings of close family members. The Sarawak Chinese wore silver ornaments similar to those produced by the Straits Chinese of the Peninsula. Chinese workmanship distinctively displayed patterns of symbolic significance. Although the smith adopted the style of ornaments worn by the Malays, he embellished them with Chinese scrolls, mythical birds and beasts like the phoenix, as well as the crab, stork, fish, plum blossom, peony, lotus and chrysanthemum. Some of the silverware of old also displayed legendary Taoist and Buddhist figures.

Hallmarking silver has never been practised in this country to guarantee the standard silver content of the products. However, a move in this direction has been made by the Malaysian Handicraft Development Corporation in order to comply with international standards. At the moment a buyer has no guarantee of the quality of Malaysian silverware and purchases it not for the intrinsic worth of the silver content but for the skill that has gone into producing a piece of artistic value.

THESE PAGES:
TWO BEAUTIFUL SILVER
GILT *TEPAK SIREH* SETS IN
THE CHINESE PERANAKAN
STYLE. THE *TEPAK SIREH* IS
USED BY THE MALAY,
PERANAKAN AND INDIAN
COMMUNITIES IN
MALAYSIA FOR SOCIAL
COMMUNICATION. FOR
EXAMPLE, IT IS CUSTOM-
ARY FOR A SUITOR
TO ANNOUNCE HIS
INTENTIONS TO HIS
PROSPECTIVE WIFE'S
PARENTS BY SENDING A
COMPLETE *TEPAK SIREH*
TO THEM THROUGH A
TRUSTED INTERMEDIARY.
THE ACCEPTANCE OF
THE GIFT SIGNIFIES
AGREEMENT TO
THE BETROTHAL.
THE SET ON THE RIGHT IS
AN EXAMPLE OF
SILVERWARE FOREIGN TO
MALAYSIA, BUT WHICH
HAS THE PATTERNS AND
MOTIFS COMMON TO
THE REGION.
FOLLOWING PAGES: AN
OGIVAL GOLD BELT
BUCKLE EMBOSSED WITH
CURLING PLANT
TENDRILS, WHICH
SUPPORT A PROFUSION
OF FLOWERS STUDDED
WITH A VARIETY OF
COLOURED GEMS
MOUNTED IN BOX
SETTINGS. THE PETALS OF
THE LOTUS BLOSSOM IN
THE CENTRE ARE
FASHIONED IN GOLD
WIRE. ON THE LEFT IS
ANOTHER GOOD
EXAMPLE OF A BELT
BUCKLE OF SIMILAR
DESIGN BUT
FASHIONED IN SILVER.

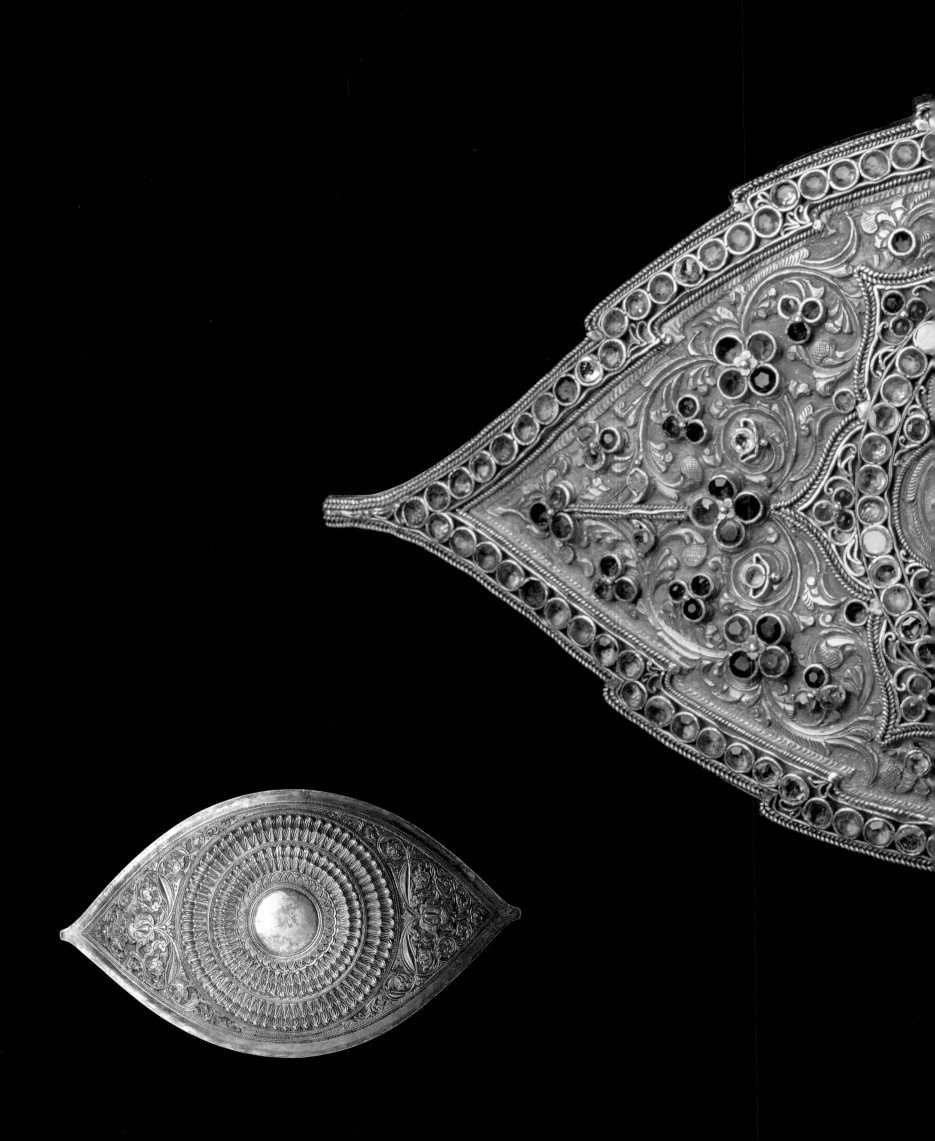

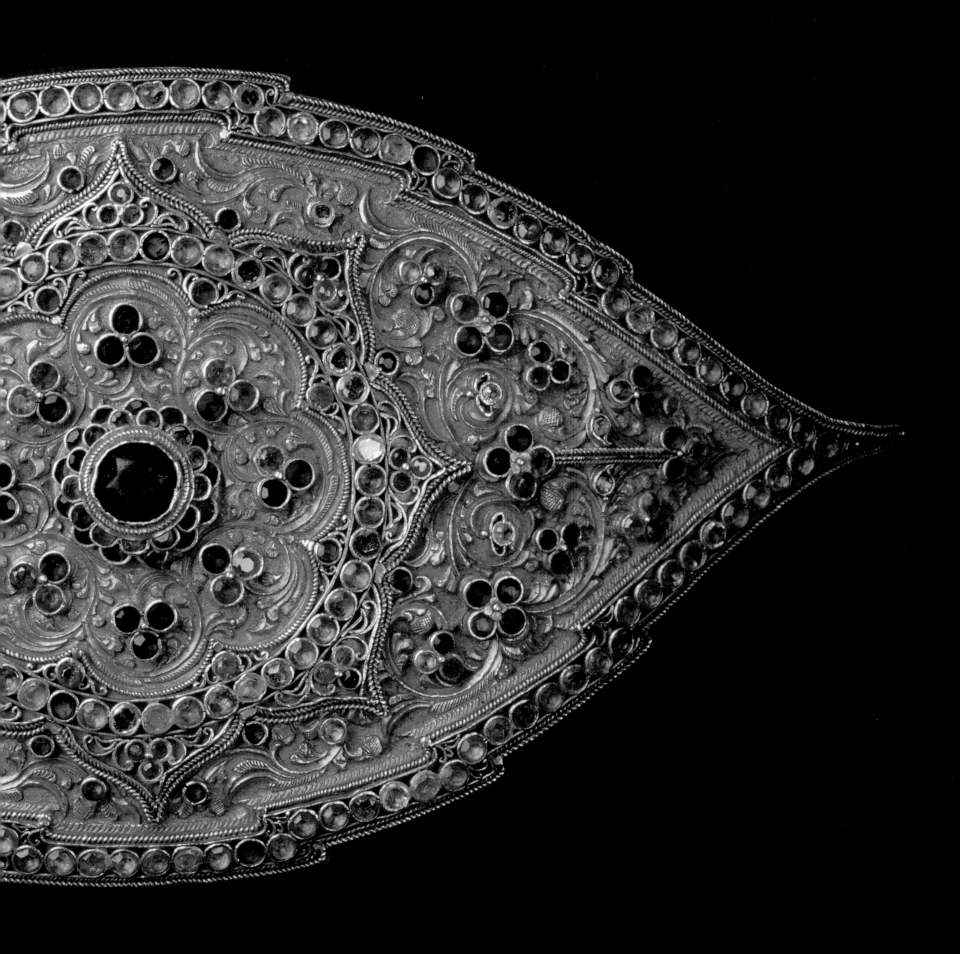

A SELECTION OF
SILVER JEWELLERY AND
ORNAMENTS OF THE TYPE
USED BY PERANAKAN
LADIES. SUCH ITEMS OF
JEWELLERY WERE WORN
NOT ONLY TO ENHANCE
THE APPEARANCE OF THE
WEARER BUT ALSO AS A
DISPLAY OF WEALTH.
AMONG THE ITEMS
COMMONLY USED ARE
COMBS, PENDANTS,
BLOUSE PINS, HAIR PINS,
RINGS, BANGLES,
EARRINGS AND BELTS
WITH DECORATIVE
BUCKLES.

A GOLDSMITH
CONCENTRATING ON
PUTTING THE FINAL
TOUCHES TO THE
CLASP OF A FINGER
RING BEFORE THE
GEMSTONE IS SET INTO
THE BEZEL — A VERY
LABORIOUS AND TIME-
CONSUMING TASK.

A SILVERSMITH, WITH
HIS HOMEMADE TOOLS
AT HIS BENCH, USING A
SMALL HAMMER AND A
PUNCH MADE OF STEEL.
THIS TYPE OF WORK
REQUIRES A GREAT DEAL
OF CONCENTRATION AND
PRECISION TO ENSURE
THAT A UNIFORM
PATTERN IS ACHIEVED.
AN ARTICLE SUCH AS
THIS MAY TAKE THE
SILVERSMITH ABOUT A
WEEK TO COMPLETE.

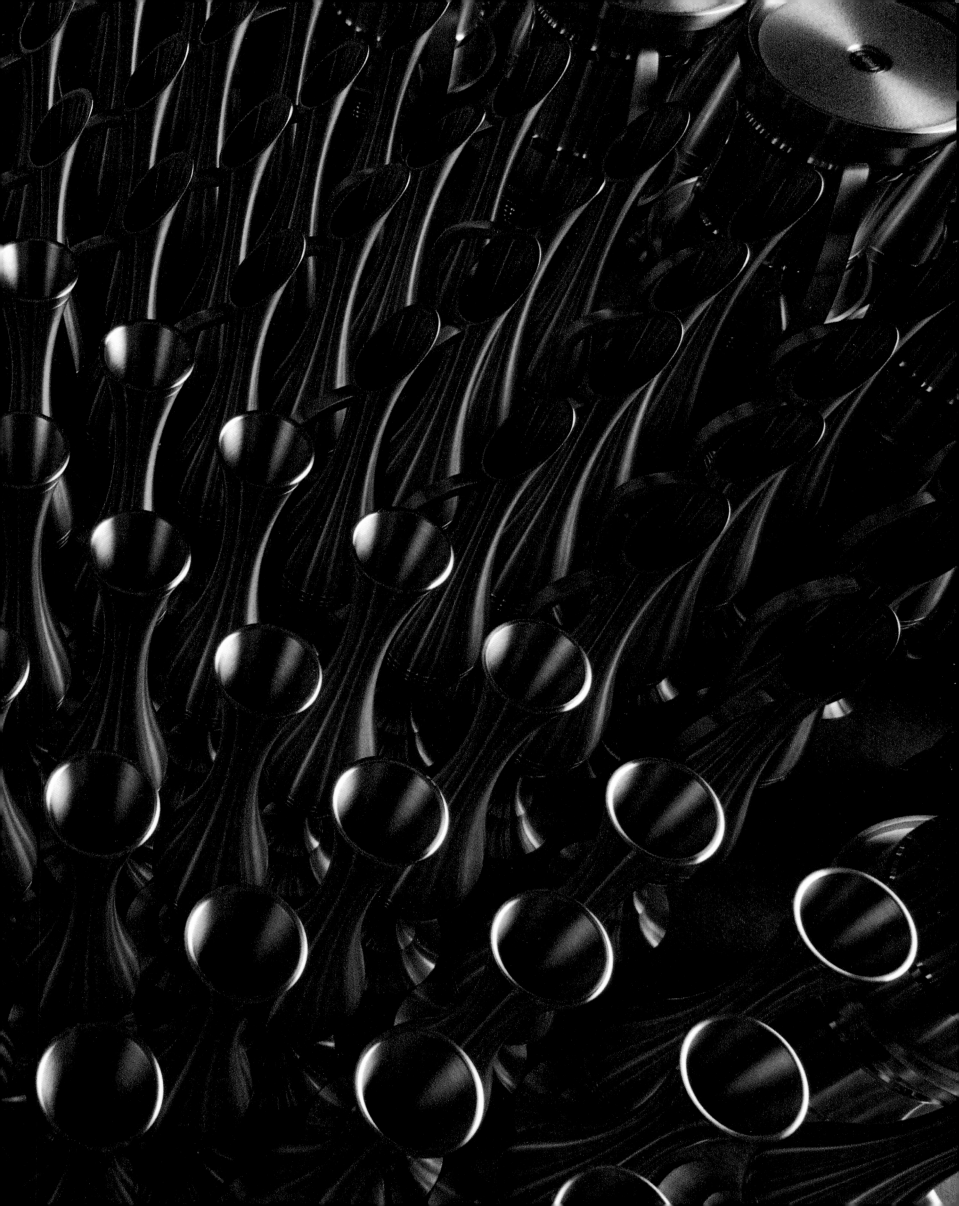

PEWTER

Pewter is an alloy mainly composed of tin strengthened by the addition of small amounts of other metals, and has been in domestic use for thousands of years. After platinum, gold and silver, it ranks as the world's fourth most highly prized commercial metal and has long been an important source of revenue for Malaysia. It has been mined in the Peninsula for over six hundred years, and has successively been sought after by the Javanese Majapahit empire, the Melaka Sultanate, the Portuguese, Dutch and British.

The most highly concentrated tin deposits are located in the states of Perak, Selangor and Pahang. In the beginning, the ore was obtained by panning small recesses along riverbanks. It was not until the 19th century when rich surface deposits were exhausted that miners had to resort to mechanical methods. The first major reform came with the introduction of pumps to force jets of water on to the pit face to break up the surface into a slurry of mud and water. In order to filter the mixture the slurry was directed onto a diagonal wooden ramp, with upright slats set at regular intervals. As the mixture flowed down the ramp or *palong*, the tin ore, which was denser, became trapped in the slats, allowing the mud and water to drain away.

The industry was later revolutionised by the invention of the tin dredge, an enormous piece of equipment the size and shape of a paddle steamer. The dredge, which floated on water, was equipped with a revolving belt of buckets which, as they rotated, scooped up the mud at depths of up to 42m. Naturally, a machine this size produced an enormous increase in tin output.

The early pioneers, both Malay and Chinese, believed that tin was possessed by a spirit which, if handled properly, would ensure a bountiful yield from the mine. The first metal obtained from a particular site was made into the shape of an animal, for example an elephant. After the appropriate rituals had taken place these miniatures were buried underneath the king post of the newly constructed *kongsi* house in which the tin miners would live. It was believed that the power from this animal would draw the tin towards the new mine. The strength of the elephant, in particular, ensured that as long as it was underneath the king post the *kongsi* house and the tin deposits would last eternally. Other miniatures modelled in the shape of the cockerel, crocodile, tortoise and fish also played similar roles in mining rituals.

There are no written records which can establish beyond all doubt when tin was first worked into articles for domestic use in Malaysia. Still, it is clear that by the beginning of the 15th century, solid tin ingots known as *tampang* were cast in several states, and used as a form of currency. In Pahang, with the passage of time, the plain solid blocks of tin became hollowed out until they eventually took on the appearance of an angular shaped hat, earning the name 'tin hat money'. They were inscribed with Jawi script and a decorative floral pattern taken from the mangosteen fruit.

In Melaka, currency in the form of tin blocks became obsolete with the introduction of the first tin coin that was minted instead of cast. This was the *casha* — a most magnificent tin coin, issued during the reign of Sultan Muzaffar Shah (1445-56). The coin was impressed with his name in Jawi/Arabic script and an interlaced Arabic inscription, 'helper of the world and of the religion of Islam'. After the arrival of the Portuguese in Melaka in 1511, a more comprehensive coinage was established, three of which —

the *bastardos, soldos* and *dineros* — were made in pewter. During the 16th century, domestic pewter was in popular use in all parts of Europe, as a substitute for silver. It is not unlikely, therefore, that the Portuguese also produced utilitarian and religious articles made from local pewter for their personal use. Still, no evidence of this survives today.

Another type of pewter currency which was in use in Kelantan during the 19th century was cast in the form of a money tree, individually known as *pitis*. The name was derived from the method of casting two rows of coins along a central duct which branched out along both sides. The end product resembled a tree with coins growing on the tips of the branches. In order to cast money trees, two brass moulds engraved with 15 or more recesses were clamped together. The molten pewter, when poured into the mould, ran along each recess, filling up each branch. When cool, the coins were broken off and the trunk and branches returned to the melting pot. In view of this, a complete money tree has become something of a rarity, although an example of one may be seen today in the logo adopted by the National Savings Bank of Malaysia.

Tin and the history of the industry became an important element in the development of the nation towards the end of the 19th century, when the discovery of great lodes of the metal prompted the migration of workers from China. Among these migrants was a young pewtersmith, Yong Koon, who became the founder of Malaysia's premier pewter manufacturer, Royal Selangor. In Yong Koon's day, there was hardly any division of labour, as the craftsman was solely responsible for manufacturing an item from start to finish, including casting, shaping, soldering and polishing. Initially, the tin ore would have to be mixed with lead, melted over a small charcoal brazier and manually cast into portable sheets. The sheet would later be cut to the requisite size or pattern with hand shears and hammered into shape with a wooden mallet. The article would then be filed and soldered together.

Handles, spouts, pedestals and small decorative additions were normally cast using a greenstone mould. In order to achieve satisfactory results, it was necessary for the mould to reach the correct heat before the molten tin would harden and retain the shape of the mould. The only way to achieve this was to continue the process of filling the mould with molten metal and discarding it until the desired temperature was attained.

During the early days of the industry, Chinese pewtersmiths confined themselves to producing domestic items such as teapots, kettles, jugs, tobacco boxes and religious pieces made for the altar. However, during the depression of the 1930's, many small businesses collapsed. The few surviving pewtersmiths found that in order to stay ahead, new markets had to be reached. A variety of new designs for new purposes, including coffee sets and other accoutrements of a more European lifestyle, were introduced, sometimes primarily for British and foreigner visitors, but increasingly with themes which reflected a Malaysian multi-ethnic identity.

By the mid-1940's, lead alloy in pewter was gradually replaced with antimony and copper, which rendered the pewter more tractable under high temperatures and made way for the introduction of spun pewter. Today, the production of crude tin for the pewter and other industries is

ONE OF A PAIR OF ORNAMENTAL ALTAR PIECES IN THE FORM OF A CHINESE TOWER PAVILION. THE HEXAGONAL STRUCTURE IS SURMOUNTED BY AN OPEN LOTUS WHICH ENCLOSES THE CAVITY OF THE LAMP. THE BODY IS DECORATED WITH FILIGREE DESIGNS OF AUSPICIOUS EMBLEMS, ANIMALS, BIRDS AND FLOWERS.

undertaken by large smelting firms which mix the ore with limestone and anthracite before heating the mixture at a temperature of between 1,200° and 1,400° Celsius. When all the impurities have been removed, it is cast into 100 lb (45.4kg) ingots with a purity of 99.8 percent, and marketed as Straits Refined Tin. The alloying process of turning raw tin into pewter is undertaken in enormous cauldrons, each with a capacity of half a ton of metal.

A century after the arrival of the young immigrant pewtersmith Yong Koon from China, his legacy, now administered by his grandchildren under the leadership of managing director Yong Poh Kon, has expanded to a full-scale industry employing over 500 pewtersmiths. Royal Selangor, from its 4.8 hectare location just outside Kuala Lumpur, exports pewter of the highest quality to over twenty countries and is deservedly recognised as the world's leading pewter manufacturer. A wide range of over a thousand designs are available, ranging from tableware — with a gleam comparable to the finest silver — to little collectible figurines from the world of fantasy.

Despite the expansion of Royal Selangor from a one-man business into a large-scale industry, the majority of its products are still handmade in much the same fashion as in Yong Koon's days, though on a much larger scale. The molten metal, which is now lead-free, is poured into preheated steel moulds, where it solidifies almost immediately. When the metal has cooled the item is removed from its mould and filed and polished by hand. As in the past, more complicated items are cast in several parts and soldered together so efficiently that one has difficulty detecting the join. The finished article is then polished, in some cases using the abrasive leaf of a wild tropical plant, *daun mempelas* (*Tetracera scandens*).

CONCLUSION

Despite the influx of modern factory-made products, Malaysia's handicraft industry is still very much alive. In the Peninsula, most of the home and cottage industries are still located in the East Coast states, particularly Kelantan and Terengganu, where gold, silver, brass and iron are fashioned into various ornaments and traditional weapons. Although modern tastes have had an influence on the handicraft industry, traditional methods and designs have endured with the passage of time, as have standards.

Of all the various metal industries across the country, one has set Malaysia on the world map. That, of course, is the pewter industry, notably Royal Selangor, which has become so well-established that it is internationally recognised as a world leader. Although there are several pewter manufacturers in Malaysia, none has acquired such a reputation for fine quality and workmanship. This can be attributed to the continuing research and development programmes that seek to provide excellence in content and design, and to the company's marketing strategies.

Mohd Kassim Haji Ali

ROYAL SELANGOR

IN A SHORT PERIOD OF SLIGHTLY OVER A HUNDRED YEARS, ROYAL SELANGOR HAS GROWN FROM A ONE-MAN COTTAGE INDUSTRY INTO THE WORLD'S LEADING PEWTER MANUFACTURER. THE ABOVE TOUCHMARKS SHOW THE EVOLUTION FROM YONG KOON'S *YU HE ZU XI* TOUCHMARK TO THE PRESENT DAY FORMS.

LEFT: TWO PEWTER
OBJECTS WITH SEVERAL
HOMEMADE TOOLS FOR
WORKING PEWTER.
SHALLOW DISHES ARE
MADE BY HAMMERING
FLAT DISCS OF SHEET
PEWTER INTO THE
DEPRESSIONS IN THE
WOODEN BLOCK. THE
DISCS ARE THEN
SOLDERED TOGETHER
TO FORM A COMPLETE
RECEPTACLE. DRAWINGS
ABOVE AND BELOW SHOW
DIFFERENT STAGES OF
PEWTER MAKING.

THIS PAGE:
AN INTERESTING EXAMPLE
OF A PARTICULARLY FINE
CHINESE PEWTER TEAPOT
COMMON IN THE EARLY
1900'S. THIS PIECE WAS
MADE IN SEVERAL
SEPARATE PARTS USING
GREENSTONE MOULDS
AND THEN JOINED
TOGETHER TO FORM A
COMPLETE POT. IT WAS
THIS TRADITION
OF CHINESE PEWTER
CRAFT — WHICH SPRUNG
FROM THE RICH TIN
RESOURCES IN MALAYSIA
— THAT CREATED THE
COUNTRY'S OWN PEWTER
INDUSTRY, ONE WHICH IS
WORLD-RENOWNED FOR
ITS CRAFTSMANSHIP AND
HIGH STANDARDS.
FACING PAGE:
TECHNIQUES FOR
POURING MOLTEN TIN
INTO THE MOULD.

THIS PAGE:
A SKILLED CRAFTSWOMAN
CONCENTRATES ON
REMOVING EXCESS METAL
AND SMOOTHING THE
UNEVEN SURFACE
WITHOUT DAMAGING
THE FINISHED PRODUCT.
FACING PAGE: AN AWARD-
WINNING PEWTER DESIGN
PRODUCED BY ROYAL
SELANGOR. THIS ELEGANT
TEA SET IS MADE IN A
BRILLIANT MIRROR FINISH
WHICH, AT FIRST GLANCE,
IS EASILY MISTAKEN
FOR SILVER.

OTHER CRAFTS

FACING PAGE:
KITE MAKER SAFIE
BIN JUSOH GLUEING A
COMPLETED KITE ONTO
ITS FRAME. A KITE MAY
BE MADE OF ANYTHING
FROM THREE TO
FIVE LAYERS OF
COLOURED PAPER.
THIS PAGE:
A COLOURFUL
DECORATIVE KITE
FROM KELANTAN.

RIGHT: AN IVORY *SIREH*
SET CLAD IN BEAUTIFULLY
INTRICATE SILVER WORK
WHICH HAS BEEN
CAREFULLY FASHIONED
TO FIT EACH RECEPTACLE.
THE PRACTICE OF
CHEWING BETEL LEAVES IS
CENTURIES OLD AND IS
BELIEVED TO HAVE ITS
ORIGINS IN THIS REGION.
THE CHEWING OF THE
QUID ACTS AS A
MILD STIMULANT.
BELOW: THE BEAUTIFULLY
CARVED DEER HORN HILT
OF A *PARANG ILANG*
FROM SARAWAK.

A PERANAKAN
BEADWORKER
METICULOUSLY SEWING
BEADS ONTO A TAUTLY
STRETCHED CLOTH.
BEADWORK MAY BE
USED TO DECORATE
ACCESSORIES SUCH AS
PURSES, HANDBAGS,
BELTS, TAPESTRIES
AND BEDSPREADS,
AMONG OTHERS.

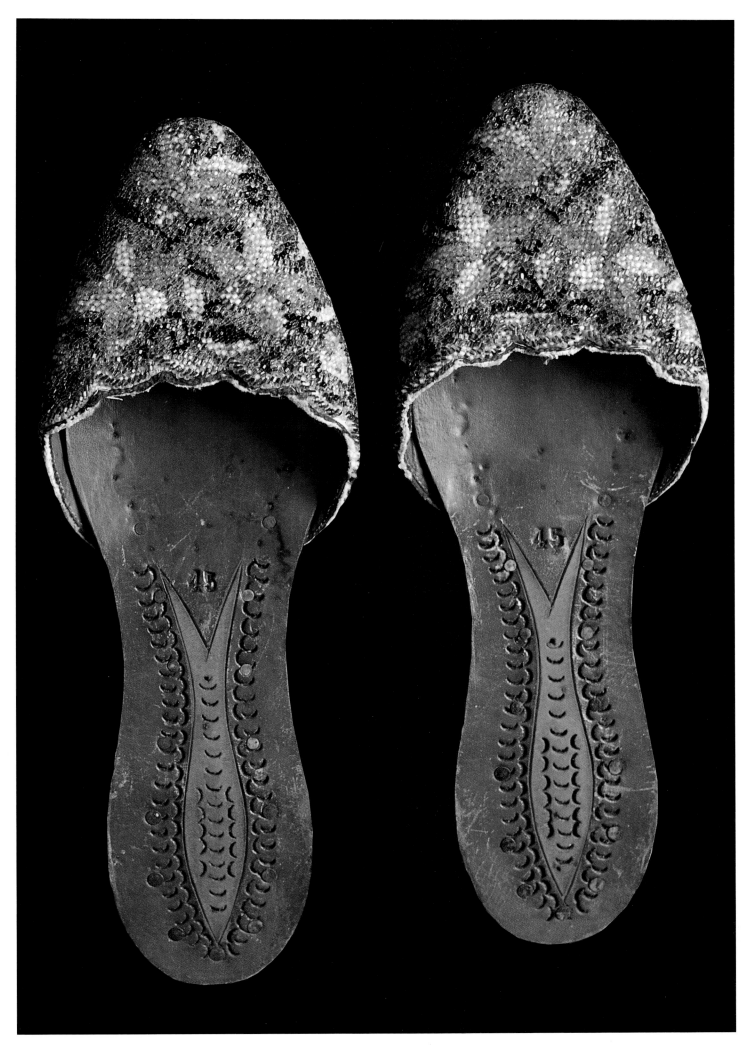

A PAIR OF BEADED
SLIPPERS CRAFTED BY
STRAITS-BORN CHINESE
WOMEN, (NONYA).
TRADITIONALLY, NONYA
WOMEN WERE TAUGHT
THE ART OF SEWING
BEADED SLIPPERS FROM
AN EARLY AGE AND
THESE ITEMS FORMED
PART OF THE MARRIAGE
TROUSSEAU. TODAY
MANY WOMEN STILL SEW
AND COLLECT THEM.

THE INTERIOR OF A SHOP IN PENANG WHICH PRODUCES CHINESE PAPER RITUAL ITEMS. THESE OBJECTS PLAY AN IMPORTANT PART IN CHINESE CEREMONIES CONNECTED WITH BIRTH, DEATH AND MARRIAGE, AS THE CHINESE BELIEVE THAT THEY MANIFEST A CONNECTION BETWEEN THIS WORLD OF HUMANS AND THE NEXT OF GODS, SPIRITS AND ANCESTORS.

A PAPER CRAFTSMAN
WORKING ON PART OF A
PAPER HOUSE FOR A *KONG
TEIK* FESTIVAL. THIS
CHINESE FESTIVAL IS
PERFORMED TO 'RAISE
CREDIT' FOR THE NEWLY
DECEASED TO SAFEGUARD
HIS PASSAGE AND STAY
IN THE AFTERWORLD.
OFFERINGS MADE
USUALLY INCLUDE A
PAPER HOUSE, PAPER
MONEY, CLOTHES AND
ACCESSORIES. THESE
ARE BURNT AFTER THE
FESTIVAL'S COMPLETION.

CRAFTS MAP OF MALAYSIA

SILVER JUG FROM SILVER
CENTRE, KELANTAN

BATIK WITH
PLANT MOTIF

PERIOK FROM KAMPUNG
MAMBONG, KELANTAN

SONGKET
TROUSERS

WAVY KRIS
BLADE

THAILAND

PERLIS

KEDAH

Ayer
Hitam

PENANG

PERAK

Kota
Bharu

Kuala
Krai

Kuala
Terengganu

KELANTAN

TERENGGANU

DECORATIVE KITE
FROM KELANTAN

BRASS CONTAINER FROM
TERENGGANU MUSEUM

Kuala
Kangsar

BEADED *NONYA*
SLIPPERS

PAHANG

Kuantan

MENGKUANG MAT

SELANGOR

Kuala Lumpur

NEGRI
SEMBILAN

Temerloh

Rembau

MELAKA

Pekan

JOHOR

CUSHION DECORATED
WITH *TEKAT* EMBROIDERY

KAIN LIMAR, A MALAY
COURTLY CLOTH

PEWTER TEAPOT FROM
ROYAL SELANGOR

DONGSON BRONZE BELL
FROM MUZIUM NEGARA

WOOD PANEL FROM
HOUSE OF REMBAU

ANTIQUE SILVER BELT
FROM MELAKA

RATTAN
CONTAINER

232

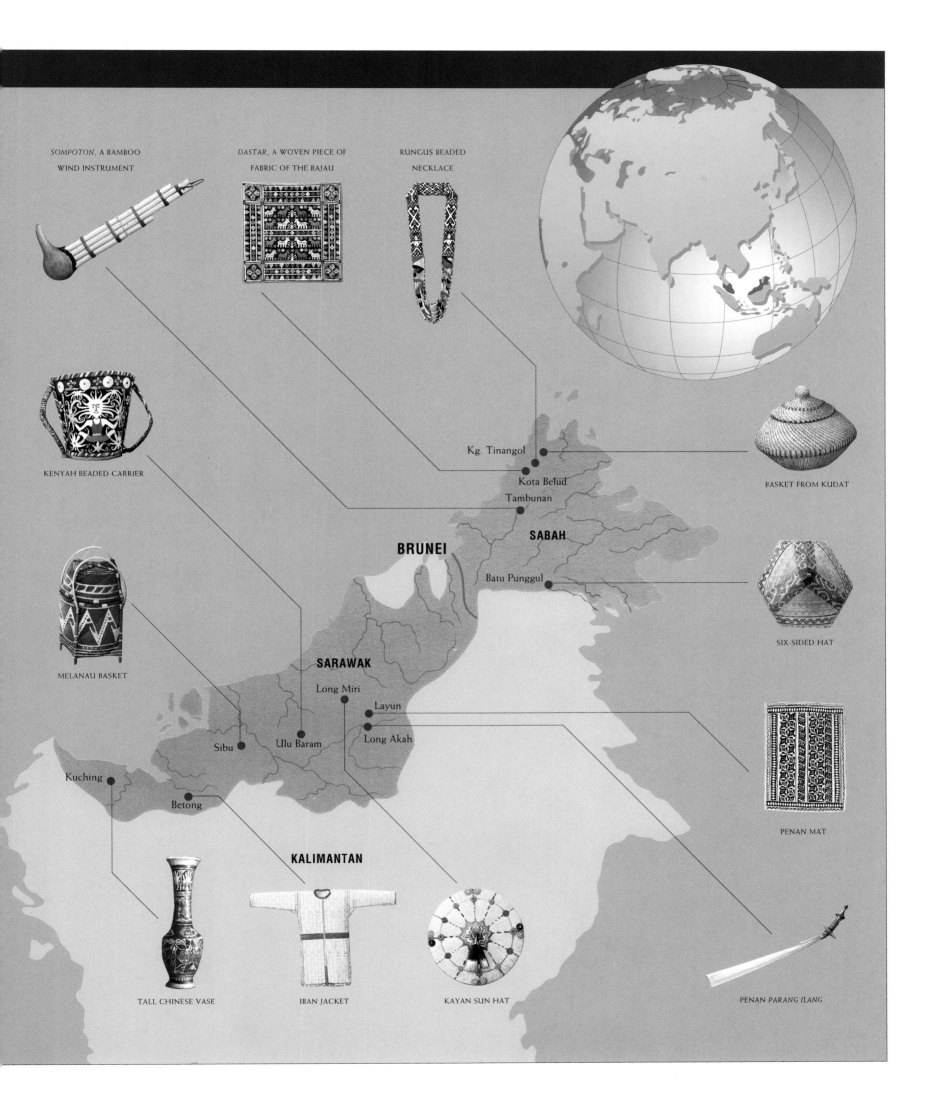

SOMPOTON, A BAMBOO
WIND INSTRUMENT

DASTAR, A WOVEN PIECE OF
FABRIC OF THE BAJAU

RUNGUS BEADED
NECKLACE

KENYAH BEADED CARRIER

MELANAU BASKET

BASKET FROM KUDAT

SIX-SIDED HAT

PENAN MAT

PENAN PARANG ILANG

Kg. Tinangol

Kota Belud

Tambunan

BRUNEI

SABAH

Batu Punggul

SARAWAK

Long Miri

Layun

Ulu Baram

Long Akah

Sibu

Kuching

Betong

KALIMANTAN

TALL CHINESE VASE

IBAN JACKET

KAYAN SUN HAT

ACKNOWLEDGEMENTS

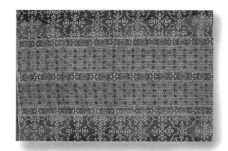

It would have been impossible to produce this book without the kind assistance and support of the very many individuals who so generously volunteered their time, energy and resources. Our thanks go, firstly, to The Regent Kuala Lumpur for its generous sponsorship of hospitality arrangements, including the book launch of **The Crafts of Malaysia**. *In* **Sarawak** *the publishers and project team would like to thank Dr Peter M. Kedit, Director, Sarawak Museum, for sharing his expertise and knowledge of Sarawak's craft traditions; Mr Ipoi Datan of Sarawak Museum for helping with the photography of museum objects; and Datin Paduka Empiang Jabu and Vernon Art Kedit for so kindly granting us access to their private collections of Iban textiles. In* **Sabah** *our thanks go to Mr Philip Biji of the Rural Development Corporation for his help in identifying and contacting key*

Sabahan craftsmen; the staff of Sabah Museum, especially Robin F. Lojiwin, Judeth John-Baptist and J.P. Guntavid for helping with research for the Fibres chapter; and Dr. Wong Khoon Meng of the Forest Research Centre, Sandakan, Sabah, for assisting with the botanical information for that chapter. In **West Malaysia** *we wish to extend special thanks to metal crafts-men En. Abu Bakar, En. Kamaruddin Che Mat and Hj. Wan Ismail for sharing their work experiences with us; the staff of the Asian Art Museum, University of Malaya for helping with research and photography for the textiles chapter; En. Hassin bin Ahyari, Perak Museum, Taiping, Dato' Mohd. Mokhtar bin Abu Bakar, Sultan Abu Bakar Museum, Pekan, Tuan Hj. Mohd. Awang Teh, En. Rusli Abdullah and En. Yusof bin Muri, all from Cawangan PKKM, Enggor, En. Misroni and staff, Cawangan PKKM, Kota Bharu, En. Ghazali Hj. Yusof, Tok Penghulu, Kampung Mambong, and Mr Tan Kee Meng, Perak Ceramics Industries Association, for their help with material for the*

Earth chapter; En. Halim Nasir and En. Mohd. Yusof Abdullah for contributing their expertise to the chapter on Wood and the Malaysian Timber Industry Board for assisting with research; Mrs Azleen Ashaari and Ms Irene Tan of Mosaique Communications for assisting with administrative arrangements; the staff of Muzium Negara, with special mention to the Photography Department staff, En. Kamarul Baharein Kassim and Ms Zubaidah for their assistance with studio photography; the various state museums for granting us access to

their collections; and Mr Michael Sweet of Antiques of the Orient, Mr John Falconer and Mr Nelson Tan for very kindly allowing us access to their archival slide collections. Our thanks also to Mr Walter Cheah of Studio Grafika for providing special insights into Malaysian crafts; En. Ismail for going beyond the call of duty and for providing unique insights and valuable assistance to photographer Tara Sosrowardoyo; and Randall (Randy) Gocke, Jit Murad, Narelle McMurtrie, Liz Tajuddin, Viv Lee, Karim Raslan, sisters Wong Mei Wan and Mei Lin, Farah Khan, Ineza and Lester for the warm-hearted hospitality they extended towards him. On a personal note, author Yeoh Jin Leng would like to thank his wife Diana for her constant support as he worked at crafting the Earth chapter. Last but not least, we would like to thank the various craftspeople featured in the book for consenting to have themselves and their works photographed, and for sharing their immense knowledge of Malaysian craft traditions with us, including YM Tengku Ismail bin Tengku Su, En. Nik Rashidin Hj. Husein, En. Norhaizah Nordin, Hj. Wan Su Othman, En. Wan Mustafa Wan Su, Tengku Ibrahim Tengku Wok, Puan Habibah Ikram and Mrs Chin of Jalan Pokok Sena, Ayer Hitam.

Dato' Haji Sulaiman Othman

Dato' Haji Sulaiman Othman is an acknowledged expert on Malaysian crafts. Presently the Director-General of the Malaysian Handicraft Development Corporation, he is also a talented crafts practitioner, having studied Industrial Design at the Mara Institute of Technology and later Fine Metal at Ulster College, Northern Ireland, where he graduated with First Class Honours. He has received meritorious awards from the Sultan of Kedah and the King of Malaysia, and is also a recipient of a cultural award from the Australian Government Department of Foreign Affairs. In 1986 he was awarded the Japan External Trade Organization (JETRO) Award for Outstanding Contribution to Import Promotion Activities.

Khoo Joo Ee

Art historian Dr. Khoo Joo Ee, author of the chapter on Textiles, received her doctorate in Southeast Asian Art and Archaeology from the University of London (School of Oriental and African Studies). The Curator of the Asian Art Museum in Kuala Lumpur, she sits on the Board of the National Art Gallery and is a founder-life member of the Penang Heritage Trust. She has numerous publications to her credit.

Vernon Art Kedit

Vernon Art Kedit, author of the essay on *pua kumbu*, comes from an old Iban family of the Saribas. A pupil of the loom himself, and descended from an ancient unbroken line of *indu tau nakar* masterweavers, Vernon is anxious to preserve the 'old knowledge'. He is particularly involved in the study of Iban weaving esotericism, and has written and lectured widely on the subject. Vernon graduated with an honours degree in law from the UK, where he also studied music.

Haji Rudin Salinger

Haji Rudin Salinger, author of the chapter on Wood, a scientist by training, holding degrees in Zoology, Chemistry and Physics, has had a long love affair with Malaysia, its cultures, craftspeople and foods. His own house, 'Rudinara', traditionally constructed of chengal wood, over a period of six and a half years, mostly without nails, is a reflection of his deep commitment to traditional craftsmanship, and to the use of wood. He has provided cultural orientations to Malaysia to both Malaysians and expatriates. Haji Rudin has travelled widely throughout the country, including the Bornean states of Sabah and Sarawak and has produced a number of documentary videos on Malaysian subjects. He has authored articles on the culture and crafts of Malaysia.

Mohd. Kassim Haji Ali

Mohd. Kassim Haji Ali, who authored the Metals chapter, studied numismatics and museology at the Department of Coins and Metals, and the Department of Ethnography of the British Museum, London. He was formerly the Curator of Ethnology and later served as Assistant Director for Supporting Services at the Department of Museums and Antiquity, Kuala Lumpur. Presently he is the First Vice-President of the Malaysian Numismatic Society and a Fellow of the Royal Numismatic Society of Great Britain. He has written many articles on arts and crafts and has co-authored five books on numismatics and a catalogue on gold jewellery and ornaments of Malaysia, as well as a coffeetable book on the same subject in Bahasa Malaysia.

Patricia Regis

Patricia Regis, author of the chapter on Fibres, is a former Director of the Sabah Museum, Kota Kinabalu. She completed her undergraduate studies in social anthropology and postgraduate museum studies in the United Kingdom. She has travelled extensively throughout Sabah documenting and recording local traditions, particularly the bridewealth system of the Murut of Pensiangan and the ritual practices and belief systems of the Lotud of Tuaran.

Siti Zainon Ismail

Siti Zainon Ismail was born in Gombak, Selangor in 1949. She studied at the Indonesian Academy of Fine Arts in Yogyakarta, and graduated with a Bachelor of Fine Arts degree in 1973. She received her Master of Arts from the National University of Malaysia in 1979, and her Ph.D. from University Malaya in 1992 for her research on Malay costumes. From 1974 to 1976, she worked as an instructor with the Malaysian Ministry of Culture, Youth and Sports. She has taught since then at the National University of Malaysia, where she is an Associate Professor. Siti Zainon is also a well-known artist and poet.

Yeoh Jin Leng

Yeoh Jin Leng, who authored the chapter on Earth, is by profession an art educationist and by vocation an artist. He was involved with art education at the Specialist Teachers' Training Institute, Cheras, for 20 years and as Dean of Studies at the Malaysian Institute of Art for 10 years. An accomplished painter and potter, he served as Guest Artist to the Federal Republic of Germany and to the U. S. in 1970, and is the recipient of numerous painting awards, including the Australian Culture Award 1990. He has participated in many regional exhibitions and written several papers on art education.

PHOTO CREDITS

Cover: Abdul Halim Mohd Noor/ Norhaizah Nordin's collection, Kg. Raja Besut, Terengganu.

Endpapers: Abdul Halim Mohd Noor/ YM Tengku Ismail bin Tengku Su's songket collection, Terengganu.

Frontispiece: courtesy of Muzium Negara.

5: Abdul Halim Mohd Noor/ textiles from Puan Azah Aziz's collection, jewellery from Muzium Seni Asia.

6-7: courtesy of Michael Sweet/ Antiques of the Orient.

Contents pages: Earth: Tara Sosrowardoyo/ Muzium Negara collection. Fibres: Lawrence Lim/ Sarawak Museum collection. Wood: Abdul Halim Mohd Noor/ Terengganu Museum collection. Textiles: courtesy of Muzium Negara. Metals: courtesy of Muzium Negara. Other crafts: courtesy of National Museum, Singapore.

10-11: Abdul Halim Mohd Noor/ Kota Bharu Permai Silverware, Kelantan.

12: Ibrahim Ahmad/ Muzium Negara collection.

13: courtesy of Muzium Negara.

14: courtesy of Nelson Tan.

15: courtesy of Bernard Durazzo.

16: courtesy of Dominic Sansoni.

17: courtesy of Dennis Lau.

19: Abdul Halim Mohd Noor/ Haji Wan Ismail's brass workshop, Terengganu.

20: Courtesy of Dennis Lau.

21: courtesy of Dennis Lau.

22: Abdul Halim Mohd Noor/ Terengganu Museum.

23: Tara Sosrowardoyo/ Kraftangan Regional Centre, Temerloh.

24-25: Tara Sosrowardoyo/ Perak Museum collection.

26: Tara Sosrowardoyo/ Kg. Kedah pottery, Bagan Serai, Perak.

28: © Editions Gallimard.

31: Tara Sosrowardoyo/ Kg. Kedah pottery, Bagan Serai, Perak.

33: Abdul Halim Mohd Noor/ Terengganu Museum collection.

35: Tara Sosrowardoyo/ Kg. Sayong pottery, Kuala Kangsar, Perak.

37 (top & bottom): Tara Sosrowardoyo/ Perak Museum collection.

38: Tara Sosrowardoyo/ Perak Museum collection.

39: Lawrence Lim/ Sarawak Museum collection.

41: Tara Sosrowardoyo/ Perak Museum collection.

42-43: Tara Sosrowardoyo/ Perak Museum collection.

44-45: Abdul Halim Mohd Noor/ Terengganu Museum collection.

45: Lawrence Lim/ Sarawak Museum collection.

46: courtesy of Kraftangan.

47: Tara Sosrowardoyo/ Kg. Sayong pottery, Kuala Kangsar, Perak.

48: Dennis Lau/ pottery in Kuching.

49: Tara Sosrowardoyo/ Kg. Kedah pottery, Bagan Seria, Perak.

50: Tara Sosrowardoyo/ Kuala Selangor pottery.

51: Tara Sosrowardoyo/ Kg. Kedah pottery, north of Bagan Serai.

52 (top): Tara Sosrowardoyo/ Asian Pottery, Penang.

52 (bottom): Tara Sosrowardoyo/ Dragon kiln, Ipoh.

53: Tara Sosrowardoyo/ Asian Pottery, Penang.

54-55: Lawrence Lim/ Vernon Art Kedit's collection.

56: courtesy of John Falconer.

58: courtesy of Michael Sweet/ Antiques of the Orient.

59: courtesy of Michael Sweet/ Antiques of the Orient.

60: Abdul Halim Mohd Noor/ Kraftangan Regional Centre, Kuala Terengganu.

62: Lawrence Lim/ Sarawak Museum collection.

63: courtesy of Michael Sweet/ Antiques of the Orient.

65: Lawrence Lim/ Sarawak Museum collection.

67: Tommy Chang/ Sabah Museum collection.

68: courtesy of Kraftangan.

69: courtesy of Kraftangan.

71: Lawrence Lim/ Sarawak Museum collection.

72-73: Dennis Lau/ Penan weaver, Layun, Baram, Sarawak.

73: Dennis Lau.

74: Tommy Chang/ weaver, Silungai longhouse, Sabah.

75: Dennis Lau/ Melanau weaver, Matu, Sarawak.

76: Dennis Lau/ Bidayuh weaver, Pedawan, Kuching.

77: Tommy Chang/ weaver, Kg Tinangol, Sabah.

78-79: courtesy of John Falconer.

79 (top & bottom): Abdul Halim Mohd Noor/ Muzium Negara collection.

80-81: Abdul Halim Mohd Noor/ Muzium Negara collection.

82-83: Abdul Halim Mohd Noor/ Norhaizah Nordin's collection, Kg. Raja Besut, Terengganu.

84: Abdul Halim Mohd Noor/ Hj. Wan Su's workshop, Terengganu.

86: © Editions Gallimard.

87: © Editions Gallimard.

89: Dennis Lau/ Berawan carver, Long Jegan, Tinjar River, Baram.

90: Illustration by Anuar Abdul Rahim.

91: Abdul Halim Mohd Noor/ Terengganu Museum collection.

92 (top): Abdul Halim Mohd Noor/ Tengku Ibrahim bin Tengku Wok's workshop, Jerteh Terengganu.

92 (bottom): Padzil Mohd. Sood/ Nik Rashidin's workshop, Kota Bharu, Kelantan.

95: Abdul Halim Mohd Noor/ Tengku Ibrahim bin Tengku Wok's workshop, Jerteh Terengganu.

97: Abdul Halim Mohd Noor/ Istana Long, Kuala Terengganu.

98: Dennis Lau/ Sarawak Museum collection.

99: courtesy of John Falconer.

100: © Editions Gallimard.

101: Tara Sosrowardoyo/ Muzium Negara collection.

102-103: Abdul Halim Mohd Noor/ Norhaizah Nordin's workshop, Kg. Raja Besut, Terengganu.

104: Tara Sosrowardoyo/ Kraftangan Regional Centre, Temerloh.

105 (top & bottom): Tara Sosrowardoyo/ Kraftangan Regional Centre, Temerloh.

106 (top): Abdul Halim Mohd Noor/ Istana Sri Menanti, Negri Sembilan.

106 (bottom): Abdul Halim Mohd Noor/ 300-year old mosque at Nilam Puri, Kelantan.

107: Abdul Halim Mohd Noor/ 300-year old mosque at Nilam Puri, Kelantan.

108-109: Abdul Halim Mohd Noor/ Bibah Songket, Kuala Terengganu.

110: Abdul Halim Mohd Noor/ textiles from Puan Azah Aziz's collection & jewellery from Muzium Seni Asia.

112-113: Illustrations by Anuar Abdul Rahim.

115: courtesy of John Falconer.

116: Abdul Halim Mohd Noor/ YM Tengku Ismail bin Tengku Su's songket workshop, Terengganu.

119: Ibrahim Ahmad/ Muzium Negara collection.

120: courtesy of John Falconer.

121: Lawrence Lim/ Collection Datin Paduka Empiang Jabu.

122-123: courtesy of John Falconer.

123: Ibrahim Ahmad/ Muzium Negara collection.

124-125: H. Lin Ho/ Muzium Seni Asia collection.

126: Ibrahim Ahmad/ Muzium Negara collection.

127: Ibrahim Ahmad/ Muzium Negara collection.

128-129: Abdul Halim Mohd Noor/ Bibah Songket, Kuala Terengganu.

130: Abdul Halim Mohd Noor/ YM Tengku Ismail bin Tengku Su's songket collection.

131: Abdul Halim Mohd Noor/ Bibah Songket, Kuala Terengganu.

132: Ibrahim Ahmad/ Puan Azah Aziz's private collection.

133: © EDM.

134: Tara Sosrowardoyo/ Penang Batik Factory.

135: Tara Sosrowardoyo/ Penang Batik Factory.

136: Abdul Halim Mohd Noor/ Yusop Batik, Kelantan.

137: Abdul Halim Mohd Noor/ Yusop Batik, Kelantan.

138: Abdul Halim Mohd Noor/ Dr Siti Zainon Ismail's private collection.

141: Ibrahim Ahmad/ Puan Azah Aziz's private collection.

142 (top): Abdul Halim Mohd Noor/ Dr Siti Zainon Ismail's private collection.

142 (bottom): Tara Sosrowardoyo/ hand of tekat maker Mrs Rofeah bte Abdul Mariaf, Kuala Kangsar, Perak.

143: Abdul Halim Mohd Noor/ Dr Siti Zainon Ismail's private collection.

144: Ibrahim Ahmad/ Puan Azah Aziz's private collection.

145: Ibrahim Ahmad/ Puan Azah Aziz's private collection.

147: Abdul Halim Mohd Noor/ Muzium Negara collection.

148-149: Lawrence Lim/ Kedit heirloom collection.

150: Lawrence Lim/ Kedit heirloom collection.

152: Lawrence Lim/ Kedit heirloom collection.

153: Lawrence Lim/ Kedit heirloom collection.

154: Lawrence Lim/ Collection Datin Paduka Empiang Jabu.

157: Lawrence Lim/ Kedit heirloom collection.

158 & 159: Lawrence Lim/ Brooke-Low Ethnographic Collection, Sarawak Museum.

160-161: Tommy Chang/ weaver, Kg. Tinangol, Sabah.

161: Tommy Chang.

162-163: Lawrence Lim/ Sarawak Museum collection.

164: Tara Sosrowardoyo/ Muzium Negara collection.

165: Tara Sosrowardoyo/ Muzium Negara collection.

166: courtesy of Kraftangan.

167: courtesy of Kraftangan.

168-169: courtesy of John Falconer.

169: Tara Sosrowardoyo/ Muzium Negara collection.

170: Abdul Halim Mohd Noor/ Terengganu Museum collection.

171: Tara Sosrowardoyo/ Muzium Negara collection.

172: Abdul Halim Mohd Noor/ Haji Wan Ismail's brassware workshop, Terengganu.

173 (top & bottom): Abdul Halim Mohd Noor/ Haji Wan Ismail's brassware workshop, Terengganu.

174-175: Abdul Halim Mohd Noor/ Istana Tele, Terengganu.

175 (top): Lawrence Lim/ Sarawak Museum collection.

175 (bottom): Abdul Halim Mohd Noor/ Muzium Negara collection.

176-177: Abdul Halim Mohd Noor/ Abu Bakar Mohd Amin's workshop, Pasir Panjang, Kuala Terengganu.

178: Illustration by Anuar Abdul Rahim.

181: Abdul Halim Mohd Noor/ Abu Bakar Mohd Amin's workshop, Pasir Panjang, Kuala Terengganu.

182: courtesy of Michael Sweet/ Antiques of the Orient.

182-183: courtesy of John Falconer.

184: Abdul Halim Mohd Noor/ Abu Bakar Mohd Amin's workshop, Pasir Panjang, Kuala Terengganu.

185: Dennis Lau/ Penan from Long Akah, Sarawak.

186-187: Abdul Halim Mohd Noor/ textiles from Puan Azah Aziz's collection and jewellery from Muzium Seni Asia.

188: Tara Sosrowardoyo/ from Mrs Chin's collection, Jalan Pokok Sena, Ayer Hitam, Penang.

190: © Editions Gallimard.

192: courtesy of John Falconer.

194: Tara Sosrowardoyo/ Muzium Negara collection.

195: Tara Sosrowardoyo/ Muzium Negara collection.

196: Abdul Halim Mohd Noor/ Terengganu Museum collection.

196-197: Abdul Halim Mohd Noor/ Terengganu Museum collection.

198: Tara Sosrowardoyo/ Muzium Negara collection.

198-199: Tara Sosrowardoyo/ Muzium Negara collection.

200-201: Abdul Halim Mohd Noor/ Muzium Seni Asia collection.

202: Abdul Halim Mohd Noor/ Mohd Amin Tukang Emas, Kuala Terengganu.

203: Abdul Halim Mohd Noor/ Kota Bharu Permai Silverware, Kelantan.

204-205: Tara Sosrowardoyo/ Penang Pewter & Metal Arts, Penang.

206: Tara Sosrowardoyo/ Muzium Negara collection.

208: courtesy of Royal Selangor.

209: courtesy of Royal Selangor.

210-211: courtesy of Royal Selangor.

211: © Editions Gallimard.

212-213: courtesy of Royal Selangor.

213 (top & bottom): Tara Sosrowardoyo/ Royal Selangor.

214: Tara Sosrowardoyo/ Royal Selangor.

215: courtesy of Royal Selangor.

216-217: Abdul Halim Mohd Noor/ wayang kulit maker Hamzah Awang Mat, Kg. Gerong Palik Bang, Kelantan.

218-219: Lawrence Lim/ Sarawak Museum collection.

220-221: Abdul Halim Mohd Noor/ wayang kulit maker Hamzah Awang Mat, Kg. Gerong Palik Bang, Kelantan.

221: © Editions Gallimard.

222-223: Abdul Halim Mohd Noor/ kite maker Safie b. Jusoh, Kg Pauh, Kota Bharu, Kelantan.

223: courtesy of Kraftangan.

224: courtesy of Nelson Tan.

224-225: Abdul Halim Mohd Noor/ Terengganu Museum collection.

226: courtesy of John Falconer.

227: Lawrence Lim/ Sarawak Museum collection.

228: Tara Sosrowardoyo/ Peranakan beadworker Mrs Chin, Jalan Pokok Sena, Ayer Hitam, Penang.

229: Tara Sosrowardoyo/ collection of Mrs Chin.

230: Tara Sosrowardoyo/ Papercraft maker, 7 Carnarvon Street, Penang.

231: Tara Sosrowardoyo/ Papercraft maker, 7 Carnarvon Street, Penang.

Abdul Halim Nasir, *Traditional Malay Wood Carving*, Dewan Bahasa dan Pustaka, Kuala Lumpur, 1987.

Alman, Elizabeth and John, *Handcraft in North Borneo*, Sabah Publishing House, Jesselton, 1963.

Alman, J. M., "Bajau Weaving", *Sarawak Museum Journal*, n.s., vol. 9, 1960: 15-16.

An Introduction to the Traditional Musical Instruments of Sabah, Department of Sabah Museum and State Archives, Kota Kinabalu, 1992.

Arney, S., *Malaysian Batik: Creating New Traditions*, Malaysian Handicraft Development Corporation, Kuala Lumpur, 1987.

Bengkel Anyaman/Tenunan dan Pewarnaan Tradisional (Traditional Weaving and Dyeing Workshop, Department of Sabah Museum and State Archives, Kota Kinabalu, 1991.

Brassware Handicrafts in East Coast Area of Malaysia, Project Report, Malaysian Handicraft Development Corporation, 1980.

Chin, Lucas, *Cultural Heritage of Sarawak*, Sarawak Museum, Kuching, 1980.

Fraser-Lu, S., *Handwoven Textiles of South-East Asia*, Oxford University Press, Singapore, 1988.

Ganjing, A. A., *Basic Iban Design: An Introduction*, Dewan Bahasa dan Pustaka, Kuala Lumpur, 1988.

Gardner, G. B., *Keris and Other Malay Weapons*, Progressive Publishing Co., Singapore, 1936.

Gavin, T., *Kayau Indu: The Warpath of the Women* (A *ngar* ritual at Entawau, Baleh in October 1988), Sarawak Museum Journal, vol. XLII no. 63 (new series), 1991.

Gittinger, M. S., *Splendid Symbols: Textiles and Tradition in Indonesia*, Textile Museum, Washington, 1979.

Gittinger, M. S., (ed.), *To Speak with Cloth: Studies in Indonesian Textiles*, Museum of Cultural History, University of California, Los Angeles, 1989.

Gullick, J. M., "A Survey of Malay Weavers and Silversmiths in Kelantan in 1951", *JMBRAS*, vol. 25, part 1, 1952: 134-48.

Haddon, A. C. & Start, L., *Iban or Sea Dayak Fabrics and their Patterns: A Descriptive Catalogue of the Iban Fabrics in the Museum of Archaeology and Ethnology*, Cambridge University Press, Cambridge, 1936.

Hill, A. H., "The Weaving Industry in Terengganu", *JMBRAS*, vol. 22, part 3, 1949: 75-84.

Heppell, M., *Whither Dyak Art?* Sawarak Museum Journal, vol. XL No. 61 (new series), special issue no. 1 part 1, 1989.

Jabu, Datin Paduka Empiang, "Pua Kumbu — The Pride of the Iban Cultural Heritage", in Chin, L. and Mashman, V. (eds), *Sarawak Cultural Legacy: A Living Tradition*, Society Atelier Sarawak, Kuching, 1991.

Jabu, Datin Paduka Empiang, *The Traditional Values and Functions of Pua Kumbu*, Sarawak Museum Journal, vol. XL, No. 61 (new series, special issue no. 4 part 1, 1989.

Lim Jee Yuan, *The Malay House: Rediscovering Malaysia's Indigenous Shelter System*, Institut Massyarakat, Pulau Pinang, 1987.

Malaysia Geographers, National Geographical Association of Malaysia, 1978.

Maxwell, R., *Textiles of Southeast Asia: Tradition, Trade and Transformation*, Oxford University Press, 1990.

Mohamad Yusof Abdullah, "Kain Limar, Pengenalan Ringkas", *Pesaka VI*, 1990: 1-4.

Mohamed Kassim, *Caping*, Museums Association of Malaysia.

Mohamed Kassim, *Gold Jewellery and Ornaments of Malaysia*, Kuala Lumpur, 1982.

Munan, Heidi, *Sarawak Crafts, Methods, Materials, and Motifs*, Oxford University Press, Singapore, 1989.

Murut Basket — Work Patterns, Sabah Museum leaflet no. 9.

Newman, Thelma R., *Contemporary Southeast Asian Arts and Crafts*, Crown Publishers, New York, 1977.

Norwani Mohd. Nawawi, *Malaysian Songket*, Dewan Bahasa dan Pustaka, Kuala Lumpur, 1989.

Ong, E., *Pua: Iban Weavings of Sarawak*, Kuching, Society Atelier Sarawak, 1986.

Pewter in Southeast Asia, Exhibition Catalogues, Selangor Pewter, 1986.

Piper, Jacqueline M., *Bamboo and Rattan, Traditional Uses and Beliefs*, Oxford University Press, Singapore, 1992.

Rentse, Anker, "A Historical Note on the Northeastern States" *JMBRAS*, vol. 20, part 1,1947.

Sellato, Bernard, *Naga dan Burong Enggang, Hornbill and Dragon, Kalimantan, Sarawak, Sabah, Brunei*, Elf Aquitaine Indonésie, 1989.

Selvanayagam, G. I., *Songket: Malaysia's Woven Treasure*, Oxford University Press, Singapore, 1990.

Serian Kelarai, Perbadanan Kemajuan Kraftangan Malaysia, Kuala Lumpur.

Shahrum Yub, *The Keris and Other Short Weapons*, Museums Association of Malaysia, 1991.

Shaw, William, *Tin and Pewter Ware*, Museums Department, States of Malaysia, Kuala Lumpur, 1970.

Shaw, William and Mohamed Kassim, *Coins of North Malaysia*, Muzium Negara, Kuala Lumpur, 1971.

Shaw, William and Mohamed Kassim, *Malacca Coins*, Muzium Negara, Kuala Lumpur, 1970.

Shaw, William and Mohamed Kassim, *Tin Hat and Animal Money*, Muzium Negara, Kuala Lumpur, 1970.

Sheppard, Mubin, *Living Crafts of Malaysia*, Times Books International, 1978.

Sheppard, Mubin, *Taman Indera, Malay Decorative Arts and Pastimes*, Oxford University Press, Kuala Lumpur, 1971.

Siti Zainon Ismail, *Percikan Seni*, Dewan Bahasa dan Pustaka, Kementerian Pendidikan Malaysia, Kuala Lumpur, 1989.

Siti Zainon Ismail, *Rekabentuk — Kraftangan Melayu Tradisi*, Dewan Bahasa dan Pustaka, Kuala Lumpur, 1986.

Veevers-Carter, W., *Riches of the Rain Forest*, Oxford University Press, Singapore, 1984.

Watters, K., *Sungkit Weaving of the Iban*, Connaisance des Arts Tribaux, 9, Geneva (n.d.).

Williams-Hunt, P. D. R., *An Introduction to the Malayan Aborigines*, Government Press, Kuala Lumpur, 1952.

Zainie, Carla, *Handcraft in Sarawak*, Borneo Literature Bureau, Kuching, 1969.

INDEX

MUSEUMS OF MALAYSIA

Muzium Negara
(National Museum)
Jalan Damansara
50566 Kuala Lumpur
Malaysia
Tel: (03) 282 6255
Fax: (03) 282 7294

Functions as a repository for Malaysia's rich cultural heritage and contains more than 10,000 items covering ethnology, archaeology and natural history.

Asian Art Museum
University of Malaya
59100 Kuala Lumpur
Malaysia
Tel: (03) 757 1066 ext 205

Exhibits cover local and Asian art objects.

Bank Negara Money Museum
Gound Floor, Block A, Bank Negara Building
Jalan Dato' Onn
50480 Kuala Lumpur
Malaysia
Tel: (03) 290 7648, 298 8044
Fax: (03) 291 2990

Collection includes coins, currency notes, tokens and other artefacts relating to the money system.

Pusat Islam Malaysia
(Islamic Exhibition Centre)
Jalan Perdana
50450 Kuala Lumpur
Tel: (03) 274 4933

Houses Islamic art objects from Malaysia and other Islamic countries.

Museum of Aboriginal Affairs, Malaysia
Km 24, Jalan Pahang
53000 Gombok
Selangor
Tel: (03) 689 2122

Displays arts and crafts objects and musical implements of the various orang asli communities.

Forestry Research Institute Malaysia Museum
Survey Research Institute
52109 Kepong
Selangor
Tel: (03) 634 2633
Fax: (03) 636 7753

Exhibits the different species of wood, their uses and products.

Lembaga Muzium Negeri Selangor
Persiaran Perdagangan
40000 Shah Alam
Selangor
Tel: (03) 559 7604, 559 0050
Fax: (03) 550 1799

Displays tribal and folk arts and crafts, and ethnographic and prehistoric artefacts.

Mara Institute of Technology (MIT) Museum and Art Gallery
40450 Shah Alam
Selangor
Tel: (03) 556 4502

Items on display include works of art by students and local artists.

Muzium Perak
Jalan Taming Sari
34000 Taiping
Perak
Tel: (05) 822 057

Has extensive collections on zoology, anthropology and local history.

Penang Museum and Art Gallery
Lebuh Farquhar
10200 Penang
Tel: (04) 613 144

Collection focusses on Chinese ethnography and customs, and the heritage of the Straits-born Chinese.

Kedah State Museum
Lebuhraya Darulaman
Bakar Bata
05100 Alor Setar
Kedah
Tel: (04) 731 162

Exhibits include ceramics, pottery, brass items and wood carvings.

Archaeological Museum
Lembah Bujang
08400 Merbok
Bedung
Kedah
Tel: (04) 472 005

Collection includes archaeological finds and cultural objects of the Bujang Valley excavation area.

Negeri Sembilan Museum
70503 Seremban
Negeri Sembilan
Tel: (06) 731 149

Displays Malay antiquities, particularly Minangkabau and Negeri Sembilan artefacts.

Malacca Cultural Museum
Kompleks Istana
75000 Melaka
Tel: (06) 220 769

Showcases the cultural heritage of the Melaka Sultanate and the various communities which have settled in the state.

Malacca Ethnography and History Museum
Stadhuys, Jalan Kota
75000 Melaka
Tel: (06) 241 934

Collection encompasses archaeology, art, ethnography, anthropology and crafts depicting Melaka's past as the seat of the Melaka Sultanate.

Lembaga Muzium Negeri
Pahang Darul Makmur
26600 Pekan
Pahang
Tel: (09) 421 371

Showcases artefacts on natural history, archaeology, ethnology and royalty.

Terengganu State Museum
Jalan Cherong Lanjut
20300 Kuala Terengganu
Terengganu
Tel: (09) 621 444

Displays archaeological, ethnographic and numismatic artefacts, and a maritime and royal heritage collection.

Kelantan State Museum
Jalan Hospital
15000 Kota Bharu
Kelantan
Tel: (09) 782 266

Showcases the state's rich range of handicrafts, silverware, songket, batik and wood carvings.

Sabah State Museum
Jalan Muzium
88000 Kota Kinabalu
Sabah
Tel: (088) 53 199/ 53 305/ 53 551
Fax: (088) 240 230

Collections encompass prehistoric anthropological artefacts of the various ethnic groups of Sabah, archaeology, ethnology and natural history.

Sarawak State Museum
Jalan Tun Abang Haji Openg
93000 Kuching
Sarawak
Tel: (082) 244 232, 244 210
Fax: (082) 246 680

Collections cover the ethnology, archaeology, natural history and local history of Sarawak.

Sibu Museum
Jalan Tun Abang Haji Openg
P. O. Box 1424
96008 Sibu
Sarawak
Tel: (084) 331 315

Exhibits depict the history and culture of the different ethnic groups residing along the Rejang River.

Bau Mini Museum
Lot 121, Jalan Lee Koi Chun
94000 Bau
Sarawak
Tel: (082) 763 433

Artefacts focus on the life, culture and traditions of the Bidayuh people.